GROWING UP IN A PENNSYLVANIA STEEL TOWN

DURING THE GREAT DEPRESSION

Edward M. Nebinger

LION BY LION
PUBLISHING

A Forecast International Company

Dedication

This book is dedicated to all of the friends who shared my growing up years in the Lehigh Valley, as well as to Americans of all ages who look back with concern to a time when our country was the world's leading industrial giant.

Acknowledgements

The Cover Photography was kindly provided by DA Visions Photography whose permission to use the image in question is gratefully acknowledged. Lion By Lion Publishing would also like to thank Robert Reinbold for his permission to use the Skyclone picture on page 43

Copyright Notice

Contents

INTRODUCTION

Bethlehem, Pennsylvania is a beautiful old town set in the heart of the Lehigh Valley, in Eastern Pennsylvania. The Valley comprises a rich and fruitful plain, formed over millennia by the Lehigh River, which runs basically east/west, with the Blue Ridge of the Appalachians to the north and South Mountain on the south side of the river. The famous Appalachian Trail runs along the crest of the Blue Ridge, with the Pocono Mountains beginning just north of the Ridge.

Bethlehem was settled in 1741 by a group called the Moravians, led by an ordained Lutheran Minister, Count Nicholas von Zinzendorf. With the Peace of Westphalia at the end of the 30 Years War, (1618 – 48), Catholicism became the official religion of Germany. However, the Reformation had produced over 200,000 dissenting Protestants in many individual split-off sects, of which a large portion were Lutherans. These were initially organized into a group known as the Unitas Fratrum, which comprised largely people from Saxony, Bohemia and

Moravia. Bohemia and Moravia were historic areas in Central Europe, comprising about two thirds of traditional Czech lands. These dissenters shared one common ambition – to be free to practice their own beliefs without interference. They accepted the Bible as their guide and practiced a code of behavior based on the principles of simplicity, purity, and brotherly love.

However, intermittent persecution over the next half century gradually whittled the group down, until Zinzendorf saw fit, in 1722, to offer the remaining holdouts sanctuary on his estates in Saxony. The Society which developed was initially entitled the Herrnhut, meaning "The Lord Watches Over," but the Count preferred to call them the Moravians, a term which gradually became the accepted name. Soon, new members began to arrive from all over Europe including, in 1725, a group of exiles from Silesia (northern Poland today.) Alarmed by the rapid rate of growth of the group, the Count of Saxony pressured Zinzendorf to stop accepting immigrants from other lands, and in 1733 forced them to leave Saxony altogether.

Attracted by exceptional religious tolerance in Pennsylvania, they purchased in 1741 a 500-acre tract of land north of Philadelphia, along the Lehigh River. There, led by Zinzendorf, the Moravians organized and built the religious communal society of Bethlehem. They also began expanding their missionary work, endeavoring to spread their beliefs to other settlements and, in particular, to the native American Indians. Evidence of their success in this endeavor may be seen by visiting the old Moravian cemetery in Bethlehem, where many of the ancient tombstones bear Indian names. Visitors to

Bethlehem can also view a rebuilt version of the first Moravian house in Bethlehem.

The settlement in Bethlehem and nearby areas of the Lehigh Valley grew steadily during the next century. A great many of the immigrants were German farmers, who found the climate and soil of the Lehigh Valley and nearby regions equal to the best lands in Germany. Because of their unique language and customs, they became known as the Pennsylvania Dutch. That, of course, was a misnomer, as they were actually Deutsch or German, and spoke a brand of Low German or Platt Deutsch.

Unlike New England, which had many fast running streams to provide power for an early growth as a manufacturing society, the Lehigh Valley, with its slow running river, remained largely agricultural until the mid-18th century. However, a number of early discoveries soon provided the genesis of what later became a great iron and steel producing area. The production of Iron and steel requires several important ingredients – iron ore, carbon (charcoal or coal, which is also the heat source), and limestone, the latter for fluxing. Through a fortunate coincidence, all of these ingredients were available in Pennsylvania.

Over the previous century various small deposits of iron ore had been found in nearby areas of Pennsylvania and western New Jersey and, as early as 1737, an iron ore mine was in operation in Cornwall, west of Bethlehem. This site later became the largest source of high- quality iron ore east of the vast Mesabi Range deposits near Lake Superior. Limestone had also been found in many locations, and large deposits of bituminous coal had spurred early iron production in Western Pennsylvania. However, for Bethlehem Steel, it was the discovery of a huge seam of anthracite (or hard coal) in the Wyoming valley, just north of the Bethlehem, which provided major stimulus to the creation of its iron and steel industry.

While early mining of iron ore and coal was limited to surface or open pit methods, by the early 18th century it had become more sophisticated and deep shafts were being sunk. This process was aided by the influx of a large wave of immigrants from Wales, Ireland and other European countries, which included many highly experienced miners.

Transportation was the next problem. In 1827 The Lehigh Barge and Navigation Company, developed by two coal entrepreneurs, began transporting coal on portions of the Lehigh River but gradually developed sections of canal to link the operation into one continuous flow. Completed in 1829, the canal was 60 feet wide at the top and 45 feet wide at the bottom, with a total of 48 lift locks over the 46-mile route from Mauch Chunk (presently Jim Thorpe) to Easton, PA. The canal boats, pulled by mules on a tow path, allowed anthracite coal to be transported to both New York and Philadelphia because of its connections to both the Morris Canal and the Delaware Division Canal, respectively.

During the great railroad building age in the post-Civil War era, canal operations were largely replaced by trains. However, the Lehigh Barge and Navigation Canal continued operating at a very low level until the early 1930s. As a youngster, the author of this book actually swam in the canal in the early thirties and sometimes visited with the lock- tenders as an occasional barge came by, pulled by mules.

The Historical Rise and Fall of Bethlehem Steel Company

The Company was founded in 1857 as the Saucona Iron Works in South Bethlehem, but several years later was renamed Bethlehem Iron Works.   Initially, it produced mostly rails and rail cars, but in response to Civil War demands, soon began producing armor plate for the U.S. Navy.   In 1899, the company assumed the name, Bethlehem Steel Company.

Charles Schwab
Source: Library of Congress

A most significant development in the history of the company took place in 1904, when Charles M. Schwab, formerly with U.S. Steel, took the helm and incorporated the company, becoming its first President and Chairman of the Board of Directors.   Under the guiding genius of Schwab, the firm began a serious of acquisitions which expanded its scope of operations dramatically.   To aid him in his task he brought in an electrical engineer, Eugene G. Grace, whose management skills complemented Schwab's ambitious expansion plans.   Together,

5

the two-man team built Bethlehem from a small producer with an ingot capacity of less than one percent of the U.S. total to the world's second-largest producer in fewer than 35 years!

In 1908 the two men staked the company's future on a new type of mill invented by Henry Grey. The Grey rolling mills produced a wide flange structural steel section that was stronger, lighter, and less expensive than the fabricated steel sections that were being used at the time. The gamble paid off, as the wide-flange sections made it possible for Bethlehem Steel to become a leading producer of steel for building skyscrapers and very large bridges.

Just before World War I, the company acquired an interest in a Chilean iron ore mine with ore of a higher quality than that available in the U.S. As a result of this acquisition, the company entered the shipbuilding business, initially producing a fleet of ore carriers, and in the process acquiring a number of shipyards. These were fortunate moves, as with the outbreak of World War I, Bethlehem Steel began building warships for Great Britain at the company's shipyards. It also filled orders for guns and munitions, armor plate, and ordnance from Britain, France, and Russia.

Eugene Grace was named President of the company in 1916, with Schwab staying on as Chairman of the Board. In that same year, bolstered by wartime profits, Bethlehem acquired American Iron and Steel Manufacturing Company, Pennsylvania Steel Company, and Maryland Steel Company.

In the years following WWI, the company continued its growth with the acquisition of Lackawanna Steel & Ordnance

Company, Midvale Steel and Ordnance Company, and Cambria Steel Company. In the years preceding the Great Depression, the company boosted its steelmaking capacity to 8.5 million tons and employed more than 60,000 people. Swab's interest in the shipbuilding business also led him to continue the acquisition of shipyards, so that during WWII the company became the largest producer of naval ships and Liberty Ship cargo carriers. During the war, Bethlehem's 15 shipyards produced a total of 1,121 ships, including battleships and other large naval ships.

While the U.S. steel industry prospered during WWII, the steel industries in Germany and Japan were devastated by Allied bombing. As a result, they had to be rebuilt after the war, and those in Germany were the beneficiary of substantial aid under the Marshall Plan. The rebuilt overseas plants incorporated more modern processes, such as continuous casting, which greatly reduced the cost of production.

Meanwhile, Bethlehem Steel, which had operated as high as 101% of capacity during WWII, was not the beneficiary of such aid, and in the crush of wartime production, had been unable to afford the luxury of shutting down portions of the plant for retooling and modernization. Nor had it been the recipient of any special economic stimulus, such as greatly accelerated depreciation allowances from the U.S. Government.

This situation was further exacerbated by the fact that, during the war, continuing demands from the Steelworker's Union had resulted in a series of concessions which were offset, in almost every case, by selective increases in the price of steel. These combined factors resulted in a significant price differential between U.S. and foreign steel.

In spite of these obstacles, the company was able to maintain a healthy rate of production in the post war decade, and actually achieved further growth, as there was a strong demand for steel to rebuild structures destroyed in the war, as well as a boom in demand for cars and household goods. Bethlehem actually built new furnaces and mills at many of its plants and by the late 1950s was capable of producing 23 million tons of steel annually.

The Bethlehem-owned shipyards were also the beneficiaries of orders for new cargo ships and supertankers, capable of cruising much faster than their predecessors. The company achieved its peak postwar year in 1957, during which it produced 19 million tons of steel and earned $190 million on sales of $2.6 billion. At the close of the decade, Bethlehem's full-time postwar employee roster at all of its plants and subsidiaries stood at 165,000.

This postwar boom, however, was only a temporary phenomenon, as the rebuilt and greatly modernized plants in Europe and Asia began coming strongly into full production by the late fifties and could easily underprice the U.S. steel companies. Another complicating factor was the emergence of many new small steel producers, termed mini-mills, which melt down scrap iron and steel in electric furnaces, at greatly reduced production costs.

The seeds of destruction had been sown, and in 1960 the United States imported more steel than it exported for the first time in the industry's history. For Bethlehem Steel, high wages, foreign competition, and the enormous costs of environmental clean-up of the lands and waters around the company's many production plants cut deeply into the company's profits and reserves.

The day of reckoning was stalled off during the decade of the seventies by two factors:

(1) The U.S. Government, in response to pleas for relief from the steel industry persuaded European and Japanese producers to cut back by 25% on the steel they were dumping in the country, and

(2) The Vietnam War stimulated demand in both the military and civil sectors of the economy. Nevertheless, the U.S. steel producers were forced to once again raise the price of steel sharply in 1969.

The author, who lived in Bethlehem, recalls periods in the seventies and eighties when it was cheaper to have foreign steel delivered in Bethlehem than to buy from Bethlehem Steel. It is significant also, that during this period many members of the United Steelworkers Union had the benefit of up to 13 weeks of vacation, due to concessions granted

In 1982, the company reported a loss of 1.5 billion U.S. dollars and was forced sell off many of its operations. Efforts were made to modernize, and profitability returned briefly in 1988, but restructuring and shutdowns continued through the 1980s and 1990s. Lighter, lower cost construction styles, not requiring the heavy structural grades produced by Bethlehem, plus increased use of aluminum and other materials, eventually caused Bethlehem Steel to discontinue steel making at its Bethlehem plant in 1995.

After roughly 140 years, production of steel in Bethlehem ceased. In 2001, Bethlehem Steel filed for bankruptcy, and in 2003, the company's remnants, including its six massive plants, were acquired by the International Steel Group. Both the coal industry and the railroads, which were greatly dependent upon the steel industry, suffered similar devastating downturns.

The Geographic and Cultural Divide of Bethlehem

Bethlehem was unique in that the Lehigh River divided the town into two distinctly different areas, which were, in fact, referred to by all of the locals as the North and South sides, respectively. That distinction was much more than a geographical one; it was also in many respects a line of cultural division in Bethlehem.

The north side of the river had no heavy industry and was primarily residential. The Steel magnates all had their mansions there, some of them looking across the river at the giant plant. North Bethlehem had been the site of the original foundation of the town, and still housed the beautiful and historic Moravian Seminary for women, as well as the Moravian Preparatory School, the Moravian church, and Moravian College (for men).

Northwest Bethlehem adjoined Allentown, which was primarily a shopping basket town, while outside of the city limits to the north and northeast, small farms extended to the foot of the

Blue Ridge Mountain and Wind Gap, which was the gateway to the Pocono Mountains, a favorite scenic area for vacationing.

In contrast, South Bethlehem was completely dominated by industry and also housed the great majority of the workers from the steel plant. This was the great melting pot, with workers from all over the world living close to the plant that employed them. The Steel Company ran for miles along the south side of the Lehigh River, all the way to Hellertown, where it had its Coking Works, which at times generated some obnoxious odors.

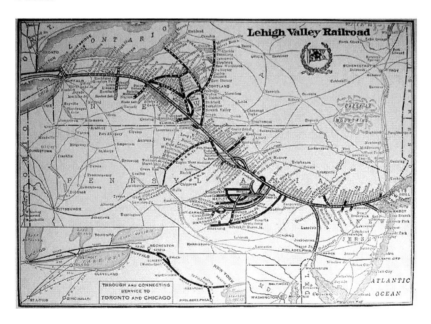

A goodly number of railroad tracks also ran along the river, many of them owned by the great Lehigh Valley Railroad. Trains brought coal from the nearby anthracite coal regions, and iron ore from the Lake Superior region, to feed the hungry blast furnaces. They delivered finished steel products to U.S.

11

customers nationwide, as well as to ports for shipping worldwide, often on company-owned ships.

Adding a further interesting dimension to Bethlehem was Lehigh University, a renowned engineering school which was (and still is) spread across South Mountain, very close to the steel plant and its (then) headquarters. A number of Lehigh graduates became executives in Bethlehem Steel, including Eugene Grace, President 1916 – 1945, and two more brilliant engineers, Howard McClintic and Charles Marshall, who built McClintic & Marshall steel in nearby Pottstown. As a subsidiary of Bethlehem Steel, McClintic Marshall provided the steel and built the magnificent Golden Gate Bridge during the thirties.

There existed, in many respects, a symbiotic relationship between Lehigh University and Bethlehem Steel. Homer Labs, which sits on top of South Mountain, received much of its early funding from the steel company and bears the name of Arthur Homer, a former President of Bethlehem Steel. This magnificent 220,000 square foot laboratory, probably the world's leading research facility on steelmaking techniques and processes, was sold to Lehigh University in 1986, when the company could no longer support it.

The steel company brought with it many things, not just employment. It brought with it a whole culture comprised of people of many nationalities who came to work in the steel (as the locals would say). It also brought with it unique foods, customs, and religions, as well as many languages. Perhaps best of all, it carried with it the unique identify of a close-knit fraternity within a little town in Pennsylvania where people shared common interests and carried within themselves a quiet pride in the industry which they supported and was a part of what made America the leading industrial nation in the world.

The Context and Perspective of this Book

I was inspired to write this narrative by my realization, late in life, of how really privileged I had been to be able to grow up in a wonderful part of America during the Great Depression. The Lehigh Valley was a beautiful, fertile area, surrounded by picturesque mountains, and populated by a talented and productive people of quite diverse ethnic and cultural backgrounds. Early cultural domination by the many so-called Pennsylvania Dutch farmers had been gradually overtaken by people of many nationalities who came as immigrants to work in the Bethlehem Steel, the nearby coal regions, and the growing railroad industries in the valley.

People in Bethlehem were proud to call themselves Americans but they liked to preserve and nourish their roots, as evidenced by the many special parks and halls which sprang up as focal points for the retention of national cultural mores. I recall Greek Park, Hungarian Park, and Windish Hall in South Bethlehem, but I know there were more. (The Windish were hill people from the mountainous regions of what was then Yugoslavia.) There was (and still is) a National Sokols Club, which I believe had its roots in the Czech region of the former Austria-Hungary, but grew to include a broader range of Slavic nations in Europe. On many Sundays I watched the National Sokols' Soccer Team practice, at a time when very few people in America played soccer. Without question, the population comprised a mixed group of national origins, but overall, these people were a solid, hard working group of Americans, as they proved by their overwhelming support of our country during WWII and subsequent conflicts.

The common denominator for most was, of course, the great Bethlehem Steel Company, which sprawled along the Lehigh River for miles and was the second largest steel producer in the world. Almost every family we knew had someone working in the steel company, and my brother and I both held several jobs in the plants prior to and after WWII.

I was born and grew up in Bethlehem, and thus experienced first-hand part of the rise and fall of the Bethlehem Steel Company, which was the engine that drove the economy of the Lehigh Valley and surrounding areas.

My father, Frank Nebinger, was a marine draftsman who was brought to Bethlehem in the early twenties from a Baltimore shipyard that had been acquired by Bethlehem Steel, and he remained a member of the company headquarters staff until his retirement in 1961. He was personally acquainted with the two great leaders, Charles Schwab and Eugene Grace, who guided the dramatic early expansion of the company.

As a boy and teenager, I recall Dad talking about various developments at the company. He was fond of telling the story of how someone once said to Schwab, "Charley, how many people are working at the Steel Company?" to which Schwab replied, "About half of them."

In the latter stages of his career, I often heard Dad saying to my mother, "I was talking to Homer on the elevator, etc." I always thought that was somebody like Homer Simpson, but later discovered it was Arthur B. Homer, who became President and Chairman, and for whom the famous Homer Labs were named.

This book starts with the earliest recollections of one whose growing up period tracked exactly the onset of the Great Depression in 1929-30, followed by the deepening of the Depression and the lean years of the early to mid- thirties, and finally the period, 1937 – 1941, just prior to WWII, when the Steel Company gradually emerged from its difficult years and the production of steel increased steadily in support of the accelerating war in Europe.

Unfortunately, this was accompanied by increasingly severe labor problems, as the Steelworkers Union sought to lift itself out of the misery of the long depression years, but in the process, perhaps overplayed its hand.

This is the story of my growing up years in that unique Pennsylvania steel town, as first seen through the eyes of a young child, then progressing though the mid years, the teenage capers, and finally to adulthood, before going off to war.

It is also the story of some of those friends and some of the events which helped shape our lives during that crucial time and the great conflict that followed.

By an interesting coincidence most of the childhood friends and acquaintances who shared adventures with me throughout the Great Depression were close enough in age so that we arrived at military enlistment age at almost precisely the time of America's entry into WWII.   In fact, I turned 18 exactly 29 days after Pearl Harbor.

Ed Nebinger

CHAPTER I

ONSET OF THE DEPRESSION

1928 – 30

Hellertown/Saucon Park

There are few, if any, steel towns left in America today. There are steel towns in India, in South Korea and in China but here in the United States, they are fading into history. Once Bethlehem in Pennsylvania was a steel town, dominated by the Bethlehem Steel Company. It has been said that towns like Bethlehem lived in the shadow of their industry. In 1928, it was indeed a very large shadow and my family was, in fact, literally living in the shadow of part of that great industry. We had a house in

Hellertown, a suburb of Bethlehem, near the entrance to Saucon Park, not far from one of the Steel properties.

In those days the Bethlehem Steel Company would dump its slag on a special company-owned hill not too far from where we were living. A line of little rail cars would appear at the top of a hill, each one carrying a hopper of molten slag. When the train stopped and all of the little hoppers tipped to empty out their contents, the entire sky lit up into a vivid pink for about an hour until the slag began to cool.

Dumping Slag
Source: Pennsylvania Museum of Steelmaking

It doesn't sound too pretty, but all things considered, it was better than it seemed, because in those days America was an industrial giant and Bethlehem Steel was the second largest steel company in the world. Now it is all gone, and all that remains are the ghostly shells of five blast furnaces, preserved, apparently, to remind people of what it used to be like.

While the view from our house toward the steel facility was not too scenic, the area where we lived was actually a "neat place" (as the kids would say), with the Saucon Creek running down into the park, lots of shade trees, and plenty of room to run and play. At that time, the shell of an old mill still stood at the entrance to the park. The flooring was gone but the floor beams

18

were still there, and the kids, including me, used to walk across the beams on a dare. My parents never knew it and I guess I was lucky, because I never fell.

Saucon Park had it all – picnic areas, baseball fields, trout fishing, a big swimming pool, lots of swings, see-saws, and hand-pushed "merry-go-rounds." The swings were very large and at first were suspended by chains, but after some kids really hurt themselves by going almost vertical and crashing, the chains were replaced with metal rods.

The little merry-go-rounds were especially popular, as the big guys would push them faster and faster until kids would start flying off if they didn't hold on tight. Of course, nothing like that will ever happen today. The world was different then; kids expected to fly off and get an occasional bruise if they were foolish enough not to hang on. That was half the fun. Nobody worried. There was no army of lawyers looking to make a quick buck for themselves and complicate people's lives.

The Park had another feature that was great - wonderful flower gardens. I don't know why a kid who was less than six years old then would still remember the name of Mr. Shelbo, the very talented Italian gardener who was responsible for the gardens, but I do. I suppose it was because my parents frequently mentioned his name and praised his talented work

The Shelbo gardens were not just beds of flowers, they were works of art. Paths wove in and out amongst the gardens, and there was always a surprise waiting around the next bend. I recall the time that Mr. Shelbo produced a complete American flag out of flowers, with alternating rows of white and red

19

flowers for stripes and the stars made up of clusters of white flowers on a blue-flower background (only 48 stars in those days).

Recently I visited the park again. All of the flower gardens are gone and the park is run down, with not much to enjoy. Of course, that was a long time ago, and facilities deteriorate. - but Bethlehem City Fathers, perhaps you should take another look. Maybe one of Mr. Shelbo's descendants is waiting.

Horses & Wagons

Hellertown Road, (now Main Street), which ran right by our house, was a narrow blacktop road. Traffic was light, mostly small commercial vehicles of some sort, although occasionally a few big trucks would pass on the way to a local delivery. The neighborhood kids particularly admired the Mack trucks, with their solid rubber tires, a great big chain on a sprocket that drove the back wheels, and a bulldog ornament on the hood. Macks were built in Allentown, about 20 miles from where we lived.

What may come as a surprise is that there were still quite a few horses and wagons plying the road. Many belonged to local farmers, but I also recall three itinerant vendors, all probably recent Italian immigrants.

First there was the Umbrella Maker, who featured a big umbrella as his sign (and his shade). People would bring out their old umbrellas and he would rebuild or repatch them until they were almost like new.

Occasionally, we would also see a tinker, with pots and pans hanging all over his wagon. It may now be hard to believe, but people actually had their pots and pans repaired; the "throw away" society had not yet arrived.

The third merchant was real popular with the kids, who called him the "Boneyman." I'm not sure why; maybe he also collected old bones, but his main business was buying old metal and newspaper, which he then resold to junkyards. The kids sold him some junk, once in a while, but never got paid much.

Of course, in the summer time, there was always the Ice Wagon, where the kids could always count on getting a free stick of ice to suck on. People would put up a little square cardboard sign in their window, with the size piece of ice they wanted indicated by whichever side of the sign was up. The choices were 10 cents, 15c, 20c and 25c. A twenty-five cent cake of ice was a very big one.

There was a dirt lane between our house and the one next door. One day a farmer drove into the lane with a wagon pulled by two horses. He stopped and went into the house, apparently for a short visit. I guess the farmer forgot to set the brake, because I was standing at the fence next to the lane and just for fun yelled, "Giddyap."

Wow, those horses starting going and I got really scared that they would run away with the wagon. Fortunately, the horses were smart, because they soon stopped and the one horse turned around and gave me an accusing, but kindly look.

Tar Babies

Unlike blacktop roads of today, which are of Macadam construction, Hellertown Road was covered with tar, and on very hot days some of the tar would melt and run off onto the side of the road in rivulets. The local kids, including me, would sometimes pick this stuff up and mold it into "tar babies." Sounds pretty grimy, but if you handled enough dirt with your paws it would start to wear off. Oddly enough, I don't recall ever being scolded by my mother for that. She must have had a high tolerance for kid tricks – or maybe I just handled enough dirt to neutralize the tar.

Many years later, when Walt Disney made the movie Song of the South featuring Uncle Remus, Brer Fox and Brer Rabbit, it brought back memories of those days. In the movie, Brer (Brother) Fox, who had been humiliated by the rabbit several times, sets a trap to catch him. It went something like this: Brer Fox makes a tar baby, clamps a hat on his head, sets him by the side of the path, and then hides in the bushes to watch. Sure enough, here comes Brer Rabbit hippity hoppin' along, and says to the Tar Baby , "Good Mawnin." – but the Tar Baby – 'He don't say nuffin'." After several such vain attempts to get a response, Brer Rabbit starts to lose his cool, and says something like, "Lookie here, I said 'Good Mawnin,' and if you don't answer, I'm going to bust you right in the chops." But de Tar Baby, "He don't say nuffin'." Finally, losing his temper completely, Brer Rabbit hauls off and hits the Tar Baby with his fists, which stick in the Tar Baby and entrap him. At this point, Brer Fox emerges from his hiding place and announces grandly that he is going to have Brer Rabbit for dinner!

It is a grand tale, and I suspect that author Joel Harris, who wrote the Uncle Remus tales in the post-Civil War era, may have also played with tar babies by the side of the road.

Jennies and Ford Tri-Motors

Hellertown Airport was just up the road from our house. I was not allowed to walk up the highway to the field, but frequently saw the old biplanes taking off and stunting overhead. One particularly daring pilot liked to do multiple loops and spins over Hellertown and all of the kids would say, "That's Keckie." I can't be sure, but I think they were referring to George Keck, who in 1937 went to Spain to fly with the Loyalist forces in the Spanish Civil War. He was later shot down, captured, and faced execution by Franco's Fascist army. The newspapers had a field day with that, and Keck managed to escape the firing

squad through some high-powered intervention by U.S. diplomats.

Airplanes fascinated me from the first time I ever saw one. I wondered how pilots steered them and came to the conclusion that they turned the wings somehow. One Sunday an air show was held at the Hellertown airport and my parents took me to the field, which was a far cry from modern airports with runways and lights. It was, in fact, a bumpy grass meadow that had some deep dips where the planes would disappear out of sight momentarily during takeoffs and landings. The airport, which disappeared years ago, was located at what is now the intersection of Interstate Highway 78 and Main Street.

Artist: John J Purdy

My first close-up view of an airplane was of a barnstormer's biplane that had large black and white squares painted all over the wings and fuselage. The barnstormer was taking people for rides, although I was not among them. I know now that his airplane was a Curtiss JN-4, affectionately known by the flying fraternity as a "Jenny," with an eight-cylinder OX-5 Liberty in-line engine. Jennies were used as trainers during WWI, , and following the war anybody with about 75 bucks could pick one up and go flying – no license required. In fact, that is how Lindbergh got his first airplane.

I noticed that whenever the planes landed they usually bounced up and down about three times before settling down on the ground, probably due to the uneven nature of the terrain. However, at the time I assumed that was how you were supposed to land. Thereafter, whenever I played with my toy airplanes every landing comprised three or four such bounces. Years later, in flight training, I learned that was definitely not a desirable technique.

They also had a big Ford Tri-Motor (Tin Goose) passenger plane at the show, and were taking people for a ride for $1. I would have given anything to go for a ride, but never even asked, as I knew my parents were not about to part with a dollar so frivolously. Instead, we settled for a free tour of the Tri-Motor airplane's cabin. One thing I noted was that it had wicker seats, which I deduced (correctly) were installed to save weight.

Interior of Ford Tri-motor

That was the day the flying bug bit me, and it never went away.

Courtesy of Aviation Week/McGraw Hill

'Speakeasies' and Bums

As a little kid I didn't know what Prohibition meant but I did know that people were not allowed to go to bars and drink whiskey or beer, but that lots of them went there anyway, including the cops. One day I heard my father telling my mother about a place called the "Chat A While Inn" which was located down the road near what later became  known as Dead Man's Curve. He was telling her how it had a little window that a man looked out of before opening the door. I don't know whether my mother ever asked him what he was doing there. If she did, I didn't hear it.

My mother, who from the earliest days was called "Mimi," was a kind lady and everyone liked her. My mother's generosity became particularly apparent around early 1930. The Depression was already closing in and lots of men were roaming the country looking for work wherever they could find it. Many of them were attracted to the Bethlehem area in the hopes of finding work at the steel mills.

It just so happened that there was a railroad overpass over the road leading into Saucon Park. Many of these men were riding the rails and jumped off near the overpass as the trains slowed to enter the city. They then naturally walked up the road toward the main highway to the steel company and consequently went right by our house. The kids all called them "bums" or "hobos" because they were pretty ragged and dirty looking and usually carried some kind of bundle tied to a stick, but I know now that those men were not bums, they were just unfortunate men. I remember talking to one of them who told me about how far he had come on the rails. Interestingly, I recall him saying that one place you wanted to steer clear of was Georgia, because if you were caught riding the rails there you were liable to end up in the Chain Gang. I guess Georgia had a low tolerance for vagrants, even during the Depression. I must add that several of my grandchildren reside there now, and it is a fine state to live in.

Frequently, one of the hobos would knock on our back door and ask my mother if she could give him something to eat. I never saw my mother turn one down, and she always told them to wait on the back steps while she looked. Mimi always managed to come up with something. I noticed she had a neat trick of keeping a large pot of gravy with leftover stew meat. Sometimes she had some fruit, but most of the time Mimi handed out a bowl of hot gravy with some bread. Sometimes there was meat and sometimes not, but the men were obviously very hungry and happy to get it, as they always thanked her profusely for her kindness.

One day some chalk-mark circles with symbols appeared on our house. According to local kid lore, they were secret signs left by the hobos to indicate that the occupant was a kind soul. While I don't know whether that was true or not, I do know that while there were lots of strangers who were fed at Mimi's back door, I never heard of any of them doing anything out of order.

Feeding complete strangers may seem like a risky business by today's standards, but things were different then.

Superheterodyne Radios

Don't ask me how a kid not even six years old could pick up this stuff but I must have had a keen ear and an interest in scientific things at an early age. Anyway, my parents had an early battery powered radio and it was going every day. The speaker was one of those big curvy megaphones that you saw on top of early phonographs, while the big wet-cell batteries and vacuum tube radio were contained in a long wooden box with a hinged lid. Oftentimes I lifted the lid to look at the works.

Superheterodyne Radio Courtesy Digicam History

Now here is the thing that I still reflect upon to this day. The radio announcer would frequently say things like "This is your powerful 50,000-watt Clear Channel Station [can't remember the call letters], operating from New Orleans, Louisiana." Sometimes it would be WJZ (New York), KYW (Chicago), or WLW (Cincinnati). The announcer also made a big deal about the fact that the broadcast was "Superheterodyne," whatever that means, and it stuck with me all these years. (Kind of like "Supercalifragilistic" from the movie *Mary Poppins*).

The astounding part of it is this; those stations came in clear as a bell and seldom faded. New Orleans was about 1,300 miles away, and Chicago about 800. Today, if you get in your car and drive 8 miles you will probably lose the puny 100-watt station you are listening to, or at the least hear two stations on the same frequency. Maybe I don't have enough facts, but I have always thought that the Federal Communications Commission (FCC) is one of our country's biggest failures! Sure, there are a lot of small stations competing for the same airwaves, but in all the time that has elapsed since the early radio days (plus the advent of FM); they surely could have done a lot better.

Walking the Tracks

Lots of times a group of us kids walked the railroad tracks. I am not sure where we were going but kids were always going or coming from someplace. One game which was constantly in play was to see how long you could walk on a rail without slipping off. It is actually a pretty good challenge, a lot tougher than the wooden balance beams that the lady gymnasts walk on so pertly.

One thing we were pretty careful about was not stepping inside of a switch track, as those things could move quickly and catch your foot. Well, would you believe it, it happened! We were walking the tracks not too far from Saucon Park and one of the kids was walking the rail by a switch when his foot slipped off and at the same time the switch went "clunk" and closed on it. The kid hollered and tried to pull his foot out, but no dice, then tried to get out of the shoe, but it was a high shoe laced all the way and he couldn't do it. We were really worried that a train might be coming.

It just so happened that there was a switch house located near the RR overpass. It was a wooden building with a window overlooking the tracks, and was set up on stilts with a winding stairway. Inside, there was a row of big levers which were operated by a switchman. I took off at a run to the switch house, which was about 500 feet away and frantically raced up the stairs. Fortunately, the operator was there and quickly found the right lever and opened the switch. Oddly enough, he did not seem to be particularly concerned and acted like it was no big deal. Maybe so, but it wasn't his foot caught in the switch track. Also, maybe he should have looked down the tracks before pulling the lever. The kid limped home with a badly bruised foot, maybe broken, but I doubt if anybody rushed him to an emergency room for a check.

You may wonder how come our parents did not know we were doing things like that. Were they careless or unconcerned? Absolutely not, all the parents that I knew were very caring people who loved their kids. But kids, like dogs, roamed free in those days. We were out playing all day; that was what kids did.   Of course, we never told our parents most of the things that went on, and people pretty much minded their own business.   It was just a freer way of life

Pot Bellied Stove

I have one final memory from that early part of my life.   Like many old homes, our house near Saucon Park did not have a furnace with vents or registers, but instead was heated by several coal fired stoves in central parts of the house, plus the kitchen range.

One winter day, after I had taken my bath I decided to go into the family room and dry off by the nice pot-bellied stove, which happened to be glowing cherry red.   The stove was located in a corner, but had sufficient room around the outside for safety.

As a typical little kid I appeared primarily in my birthday suit with only a towel wrapped around, then made a serious misjudgment and decided to walk behind the furnace to get a thorough and toasty drying.   I dropped the towel and bent to pick it up. There was a loud sssst and my posterior suddenly felt like a thousand bees had stung it!

The family had a good chuckle, as I sat on a bag of ice at dinner time.   I didn't walk behind the stove again.   Modern kids don't run that risk, but then again, they don't know the pleasure of sitting around a nice glowing coal stove, when the rest of the house is pretty cold.

West Bethlehem 1930 - 1931

Right after I started school my family moved from Hellertown to a nice apartment on Broad Street in northwest Bethlehem. It was here that the terms "Brass Ring," "Skyclone," and "Pitch a Penny" would become part of my childhood vocabulary.

Trolleys and Monkeys

The dwellers in the Lehigh Valley were fortunate to have a great trolley car transportation system, which was operated by the Lehigh Valley Transit System. Three cities – Allentown, Bethlehem and Easton – were all connected, and there were also tracks that ran to many of the surrounding suburbs, including Fountain Hill, Gauffs Hill, Farmington, and Hellertown. Our apartment fronted Broad Street and was thus directly on the main line, so our parents could go anywhere in the valley with no problem. Trolley cars were not only highly efficient, but were very economical. You could get on a trolley car, pay a fare (which I believe for a long time was 15 cents for a round trip), and through a series of transfers ride to virtually any place in the three cities. That sounds unbelievable by today's standards.

They even had a deal where you could buy a pass which was good for a week for $1, and you could ride anywhere by just showing the pass. Sometimes, after I got a little older I would borrow my parents' pass and two or three of us kids would go for a free trip to some park or movie.

How did we do it? Simple, the first kid got on the trolley, flashed the pass, then handed it out the window to the next one, etc., and we all met at the end destination. The motormen weren't stupid and once in a while would bust us, especially if we got cocky about it, but in general they were decent types who recognized that kids were kids and would forgive a little petty larceny.

While trolley cars were indeed efficient they had one weakness, which the kids loved to exploit. There was a long spring-loaded pole on each end of the trolley that had a special device that rode on the wire above to draw current for its power. We called it the "Monkey." Trolleys didn't have to turn around; they had a pole and a driver's seat on each end. They would simply reverse directions. A rope hung down from the Monkey that allowed the motorman to pull down the pole and reset it on the wire as needed.

Often after my friends and I became teenagers, and particularly on Halloween, one of us would rip out behind the trolley and pull the Monkey off the wire, just for fun. There was a nice flash, all the lights in the car went out and it stopped. The Motorman would patiently get out, pull it down again and place it on the wire. Kids can be devils for a guy trying to make an honest living.

Central Park and the Brass Rings

The Lehigh Valley Transit Company must have had some very astute management, as they noted that there was a nice piece of land right where their main trolley line crossed the line from Bethlehem into Allentown. This was an ideal spot for an amusement park, as it was readily accessible by large numbers of people, and the trolleys could haul them there. The Transit Company got title to the land somehow and built a wonderful place called Central Park. That was absolutely the best amusement park I have ever seen.

Central Park had everything. The ground sloped gradually up to a ridge with lots of great shady trees, and then fell off into a beautiful valley behind the park. The transit company built excellent paths which wove among the trees, and installed benches to rest on. The park had a large variety of stands for merchandize vendors and various games of chance, restaurants, picnic areas, fountains, and the full range of rides of all sorts. This included the "Derby Racer", a nice medium sized coaster which was thrilling for the average rider, the Old Mill, a romantic place where boats meandered thru the tunnels, then climbed up a hill and came down the other side with a huge splash. (Some older people called that the "Love Boats").

There was also a terrific "Spook House", complete with scary ghosts, floors that tilted, and confusing rooms lined with dozens of weird mirrors, so that you had a problem finding out which passage was the way out etc. We spent hours on end in Spook House and really got our money's worth. Reflecting back upon the confusion of finding your way out of mirror rooms, it occurs to me that today, OSHA or the Fire Safety people would require them to post lighted "Exit" signs, tipping the whole deal. On the other hand, however, it would not have been good to be in the Spook House if it caught fire.

Central Park also had a classic "Merry-Go-Round", or carousel, with beautifully painted horses that went up and down (as well as some fixed ones and carriages for the little kids and "sissies"), all paced by stirring music belted out loudly by a calliope in the center. Nowadays only a few of these original carousels remain in existence, and the individual horses and carriages are prized as valuable collector's items.

We have all heard the expression, "Get the Brass Ring", but that is the only place I have ever truly seen a brass ring operation. The "Merry go Round" would get up to speed, then a guy would swing out a wooden arm with a spring-equipped slot which fed rings that the daring riders could grab when they flew past, while hanging onto one of the vertical poles. Most of the rings were dull colored, but every once in a while one would be bright brass. If you got lucky and got a brass ring, that was good for another free ride on the Carousel. Lots of fun and the teen-agers really loved it.

The Skyclone

In the valley behind the main park, there was also a giant roller coaster called the "Skyclone." It was at least twice the size and height of the "Derby Racer" and was really a scary ride. Most little kids did not ride the "Skyclone" and I think they had a minimum age limit, but after a time I managed to con my way aboard and got one of the biggest scares in my early life, as the dives were almost vertical and it felt like you would fly right out. What was really weird was that sometimes the string of cars would stop at the top of one of the climbs. No problem. One of the older guys would get out, give them a push and jump back aboard. OSHA would go nuts over that today.

The Skyclone. Courtesy Robert M Reinbold, Jr.

On a relative scale I know that the "Skyclone" was old fashioned compared to some of the rides today, which have loops and rolls , but modern rides are highly engineered and built to exacting standards with steel structures. The old coasters were all wood structures that rattled and shook. They were primitive, and that was half of the fun. Of course, there were many rides for the little tots, as well as see-saws and swings galore. For the older people the park featured a full sized bowling alley, a pool room and other adult games such as Skeet, and a bar that served beer. There was also a complete outdoor theatre with a bandshell and stage, where well known entertainers performed.

The Great Shoe Caper

I knew a kid named Johnny Schuster (I am not sure of the spelling today) who had a part time job on Saturdays at Central Park. Johnny was about ten years old, and worked at a stand called "Pitch a Penny" where clients would line up and toss pennies at various targets. If they scored they might win a stuffed animal etc. Of course, the odds of winning were pretty tough and it was a rare player who actually got a prize - but it was all in good clean fun and everybody had a smile on his face, particularly the owner. Anyway, the pennies that missed fell down under the layout and Johnny's job was to crawl underneath periodically, retrieve the pennies and pour them into a large container.

We knew that Johnny worked until 5:30, so one Saturday after a fun day at the Park, a couple of us kids waited for him to finish his shift. Right at quitting time Johnny popped up from under the stand, dumped a big bunch of pennies into the container, said goodbye to the owner, and joined us for the walk home. He was wearing a pair of those high shoes that a lot of kids wore those days. I don't know why, but we called them Brogans. First thing we noticed was that Johnny was limping. We said, "How come you're limping, Johnny?" but he didn't answer and just kept walking down the hill toward the exit. As

38

soon as we got out of sight Johnny stopped under a big tree, took off his shoes and dumped out a ton of pennies! They say that Americans have always had a unique entrepreneurial spirit; I guess Johnny got an early start!

Matches and Nitrate Don't Mix

One day I was sitting in second grade at the Rosemont School, right up the street from our house, when a bunch of fire engines raced by with sirens wailing and horns blasting. The kid next to me said, with a worried look on his face, "Gee, I hope it isn't my house." "Don't be stupid," I retorted, and went on with my schoolwork. The kid was not stupid; I was, because when I got home I discovered it was my house that had gone up in flames!

Cellulose nitrate film is pretty tough and was used in early movie films. It was also highly inflammable and chemically unstable. Many classic films have been lost as a result and film preservation organizations are working hard to save these precious early movies by recording them on to more stable media..

It seems that my older brother had been kept home from school that day for some illness, and was roaming around looking for something in a bedroom closet. My father had an early motion picture projector, with a large box full of reels of that early nitrate film that was very flammable. There was no light in the closet so my brother lit a match and held it while he was looking. It burned his finger and he dropped the match – right into the box of film, of which some was loose on the reels Whoosh, the film went up, the dresses in the closet caught fire, then the bedding and drapes in the bedroom and we were off to the races.

That took care of the apartment on Broad Street in West Bethlehem.

Chapter II

THE DEPRESSION DEEPENS

1931 – 1932

Hanover Street

After the fire my parents found a little house on Hanover Street in West Bethlehem, near the Hill to Hill Bridge. Mimi liked it because it had a nice lawn, shady trees, and a plot for a garden in the back.

It was an interesting place to live, because there were lots of kids my age or older and we never lacked for something to do. There was an armory about a block away, where the soldiers from the Army Coast Artillery sometimes drilled with their band playing, and on every summer weekend there was a massive kite flying bash which took place behind the armory, with kites of all types soaring out over the city. Hardly anybody bought their kites, they made their own. They were easy to make with a few sticks, some colored tissue paper, string, and some glue made out of flour and water.

Nipsi

One street game we quickly learned to play was called Nipsi. I have never since met anyone who played Nipsi, but for us it was the only game. Kind of like Stick Ball that a lot of New York kids grew up on, but the only relationship between that and Nipsi was the stick. The way it worked, you got a broomstick and sawed off a piece about five inches long. You then sharpened this piece on both ends and it became the Nipsi.

A piece of the broomstick handle then served as the bat and the play went as follows: You set the Nipsi down and tapped on the pointed end with the stick, causing it to fly into the air spinning, at which point you whacked it as hard as you could with the bat, sending it flying down the street. The other kids would do all in their power to stop the flying Nipsi, kind of like catching a fly, except that the Nipsi was pointed and we were not wearing gloves. A few punctures happened but usually the point got dulled anyway.

The batter then laid his stick on the ground and the fielders threw the Nipsi at the stick. If one of them hit it the batter was out. If not, he then got three chances to score by hitting the Nipsi from exactly where it lay and whacking it, then advancing and doing that two more times. Thus, the rhythm was Tap, Whack; Tap, Whack; and Tap, Whack. However, if he tapped and the Nipsi didn't fly up that counted as one, or if he swung and missed that was hard luck. Finally, after he had his three shots you measured the score by the number of stick lengths the Nipsi landed from the batter's box. Simple, huh.

Where did the name come from? It sounds like an Indian word and maybe it was, but I don't recall ever hearing of any Indians playing Nipsi. They did play La Crosse, but that name had a French derivation.

Those games sure worked up a sweat, but we could always count on getting a nice cold drink at my house. My mother, who everyone called "Mimi", made root beer and birch beer. She had a big crock and bought the extract, then boiled up a bunch of water and dumped it into the crock with the extract, sugar and some yeast.

We had saved up a lot of old soda bottles (very carefully washed out) and used a bottle capper. To finish the job, you put the cap into the capper, set the capper on the bottle top and banged it with a hammer. We then laid the bottles on their sides in the yard so that the sunlight could start the percolation process.

After a couple of days those things were ready to drink – and that stuff was great! It had far more pizzazz than wimpy sodas and would actually fizz in your nose. Modern root beer and birch beer don't hold a candle to Mimi's real Old Fashioned Root Beer!

Migs and the Laws of Confiscation

Another game that we often played was Marbles, which we called "Migs." I am not talking about games like Chinese Checkers that are simply played using marbles, but old-fashioned Marbles where everybody put a couple of marbles into a ring drawn in the dirt, and each kid took his turn trying to knock them out with his "shooter." If you knocked any out you got to keep them, and took another turn. If you missed, you lost your turn.

There were several types of marbles. The cheapest and most common ones were made of clay. These tended to be plain-colored and were called "commies," maybe because they were, in fact, common. Anyway, the good marbles were made out of glass of many colors, and were called "aggies" (short for agates, I presume). For shooters most kids used a big aggie of some sort, but the kings of the shooters were steel ball bearings, which we called "steelies." These were prized because you could put a tremendous wallop behind a steelie and bowl everything out of your way. Sometimes we'd go down to a junkyard and pry some steelies from old vehicles. There was a limit, however, on just how big a steelie you could use.

Marbles was a game with strict rules. First, when you were ready to shoot you had to have part of your hand in contact with the ground and you could not move your hand forward when you shot. If you did, that was called "hunching" and you lost your turn. I became a pretty hot shot with marbles and could usually nail a marble 2 or more feet away on the first shot – without hunching.

Like everything else in life, Migs had its scams and perils. The old rules of "survival of the fittest" and "might makes right" were always in full swing. Sometimes, right in the middle of a peaceful game, some of the bigger kids would come along and yell "United States" and grab everybody's marbles. They got away with it because they had the power, and nobody ran home and whined, as that would have made you a "sissy." That was just the way it was, and if you were robbed, that was just hard luck.

Thinking back, I find it curious that they would always yell "United States" before grabbing all the marbles, as that is eerily similar to the way the Internal Revenue Service operates today. The only difference is that the IRS agents don't yell anything, they just take it. Who knows; maybe one of those big kids grew up to become IRS Commissioner.

The Opportunity Room; Dodging Traffic

I had transferred to the second grade at Fairview Elementary and I guess it was a typical Bethlehem school. However, one thing that set it apart from the other schools was that Fairview had a classroom on which there was a sign which said "OPPORTUNITY ROOM." The first thing everybody noticed was that the kids in that room were all weird, nerdy or downright nuts. I guess political correctness was in its infancy in those days, but one thing was clear and effective – you didn't ever want to get sent to the Opportunity Room!

Another kid and I went home for lunch one day (about a block and a half away) – no buses or cafeterias then. You walked and packed a brownbag, or zipped home for a bite. The kid and I were kind of late coming back and we ripped across Prospect Avenue without looking at the traffic. A big car screeched its brakes and missed me, but hit the other kid, who went flying. The people rushed out in a panic and took him away but I just kept running to the school.

Knowing we had done something wrong, I did not say a word until the teacher asked, "Has anyone seen William?" at which point I sheepishly muttered, "Yeah, he got hit by a car." "What?" the teacher yelled, turned ashen pale and rushed out of the room. The kid was not badly hurt; he broke six fingers.

Running the Gauntlet

There were a couple of rotten big kids in the neighborhood who kept giving some of us a hard time. I don't know why, I guess just because they were bigger and could. One of their tricks was to catch us on the way home from school. One day we came out of school and there were three of them waiting. We ran like hell for about two blocks with them coming after us, and then darted into a candy store. We said to the guy, "Do you have a back door?" He was wise and pointed, and we ripped out and escaped.

A lot of the alleys were not paved and there were plenty of cobble stones around. Every time we didn't have anything more important to do we threw stones at poles, signs, or anything. I became a real deadeye as a stone thrower and it

46

really came in handy. One Saturday one of those big kids trapped me in an alley. I started to run but I knew he was going to catch me, so I stopped and picked up a stone and threw it right at him. My first shot hit him right in the forehead between the eyes and blood spurted out all over his face. The kid started crying and ran home to his mother.

I worried some about the repercussions but they never happened. Maybe his mother thought he deserved it.

Scrammy Junior

Hanover Street was on a hill, which ran down to Spring Street, which in turn ran way down under the Hill to Hill bridge. That gave us a long stretch to try out wagons, scooters and such. One thing we got into was making skateboards, which were a plank with a couple of roller skate trucks nailed onto them.

Those things were not so hot so we soon graduated to building race cars. These were early versions of soap box racers; the sophisticated Soap Box derby cars were still years in the future. Anyway, the basic drill was to nail together a frame with a box and some old wagon wheels. Early models had just a rope to steer it with but after a while we figured out how to hook it up to a steering wheel and even rigged a brake for one of the back wheels.

Artist: John J Purdy

My older brother, Bob, and I had one car that was our proudest creation. We named it "Scrammy Junior," which I think was copied after a race horse in the funny paper strip called "Barney Google." The frosting on the cake was when we came up with the idea of putting an exhaust pipe on our car. We got a big chunk of pipe which was open in both the front and the back and strapped it onto the side. Than we got some oily rags and stuffed them into the front of the pipe and lit them. It was really "neat" (as the kids would say) to go ripping down the hill, screech around the corner onto Spring Street, and roar all the way down under the Hill-to-Hill Bridge, all the while with black smoke coming out of Scrammy Junior's tail pipe.

I guess that on a relative scale the Soap Box Derby cars of today are Ferraris as compared to our Model T's, but ours were more street worthy and I think we had more fun.

Some years later, I watched some of the Soap Box Derbies in the movies and on television. One thing I picked up was that most of the parts for the cars came in kits and it appeared that there was not much the kids had to do, as their fathers did most of the assembly. I also noticed that some of the kids did not really seem to be into it, and were doing it only to please their parents, who were the ones that enjoyed it most. This probably sounds like sour grapes – and I guess it is.

Graf Zeppelin and Dornier Do-X

The Graf Zeppelin: Source Deutsche Bundesarchive

One day as I was standing in our back yard, the air starting pulsating with the sound of many heavy engines aloft. I looked up and there above me was a giant silver airship sailing majestically over the city. It was Germany's *Graf Zeppelin*, which made many trips across the ocean safely without incident before being retired in 1937. I assume that the Zeppelin was on its way from New York to Philadelphia, or possibly to Lakehurst, New Jersey, where the airships docked. Some years later, when the disastrous *Hindenburg* fire took place, I was reminded of that memorable day.

The Dornier Do-X. Source: Deutsche Bundesarchive

Around the same time, I was also stunned to see a giant airplane with many engines flying over Bethlehem. It was at a fairly low altitude and the continuous roaring of its engines was so loud that the entire ground trembled. Surprisingly, my older brother, who also had an interest in airplanes, knew what it was and said, "That's the Do-X."

He was right. It was Germany's experimental *Dornier Do-X*, a 12-engined flying boat that weighed 56 metric tons (about 124,000 pounds) and was, in fact, the second largest airplane ever built at the time. (Russia's *Maxim Gorky* was larger, but not heavier.)

It was 1932 and Hitler was pushing the frontiers of aviation to send a message to the world that Germany was the leader of this technology. The Do-X, which was one of three prototypes, was originally powered by 12 Siemens-built radial engines of 524 hp each, but these proved inadequate and were later replaced by 610 hp Curtiss Conqueror 12 cylinder in-line water-cooled engines.

Like the *Graf Zeppelin,* the Do-X was targeted at Trans-Atlantic passenger service, with Deutsche Lufthansa slated to be the first user. The great flying boat had been on a multi-country demonstration tour, but spent many months at Glenn Curtiss Airport (which later became LaGuardia) so that the engines could be overhauled. I probably saw it during one of many test flights in the area.

Hitler's plan was unsuccessful, as the aircraft was lacking in performance and reliability. Further exacerbating the situation was the fact that the great Depression was deepening worldwide, and Lufthansa's trans-ocean operations had come under severe economic pressures.

Slow Down at the Steel Company (Layoffs and Cutbacks)

It was at Hanover Street that I first began to realize the meaning of the word "Depression," as I saw first-hand that some people were having to struggle.

While Hitler was feeling his oats and beginning to flex his muscles across the ocean, things weren't going so well in Bethlehem. Almost everyone around us worked in one of the steel shops, and the word was out that half of the blast furnaces were being shut down and layoffs were imminent.

My parents had become friendly with the Gieske family, which lived a short block away. Mrs. Gieske and Mimi shared lots of gardening lore and Mr. Gieske was a nice guy. They had three kids, of which the ages of the two oldest boys paralleled those of my brother and myself, so we spent a lot to time together.

One day I was visiting them and the kids insisted I stay for supper. I could tell that the parents were not eager about it but the kids kept insisting so I remained.

Supper was kind of a somber affair; the parents were not their usual jovial selves, and I could see that something was bothering them. It turned out that Mr. Gieske, who worked in one of the Steel shops, had just been cut back to two days a week.

From hanging out with the kids, I knew that the Gieskes bought most of their groceries from a small local grocer and that he carried them on a tab. (Supermarkets were a thing of the future). From going to the store with their kids, I also knew that Mr. Gieske paid his grocery bill every pay day.

The next day, I happened to be in that store and heard Mr. Gieske asking the Grocer if he could extend his tab a little longer. It came home to me then, for the first time, that some people were already having very tough going. There was no such thing as unemployment compensation.

Actually, it could have been worse. While some complete layoffs did take place, the Steel Company was pretty good about it. Instead of laying off lots of people completely, they elected instead to cut many workers back to two or three days per week, so that they could at least work enough to keep food on the table. This was a wise and compassionate plan, which I think was never fully appreciated by the townspeople.

Mumbley Peg

Every kid at that time had a pocket knife. A favorite game that everybody played with their knives was called "Mumbley Peg," so named because the loser had to pull a wooden peg out of the ground with his teeth after each of the other kids took a couple of whacks at driving the peg in with the handle of their pocket knives.

The game involved 15 separate challenges that you had to complete sequentially with your knife. Successful completion of each required that the knife be sticking in the ground, handle end up, with at least two fingers' clearance between the handle and the earth. Each kid took his turn and tried to complete as many challenges as possible without missing any. If you missed, you lost your turn to the next kid.

The 15 challenges were as follows:

(These first 4 were really easy.)

1. From a kneeling position, hold knife in palm of right hand with blade pointing forward and give it a simple toss up and over so that the point sticks into the ground. (Don't forget to pull your hand away before the knife drops.)

2. Same, except knife is held flat on the back of the right hand.

3 & 4: Repeat steps 1 & 2 with the left hand.

(These next 8 were a little harder.)

5. From standing position, balance knife with point down on right wrist and let it fall with one turn into ground.

6. Same as 5 from right elbow.

7. Same as 5 from right shoulder.

8, 9, & 10: Repeat 5, 6 & 7 from left side.

11. Hold knife at belly button and let drop.

12. Same as 11, from chin.

(Here is where it became more difficult.)

13. From a sitting position, hold knife blade in right hand with handle pointing forward and toss it backward over your head.

14.   Same as 13, for left hand.

15.   "Jump the Fence" – Stick knife blade lightly into the ground, leaning slightly to the right.   Hold left hand on the ground, simulating a fence.   With right hand, give the knife a swipe, causing it to jump over the fence, rotate, and stick into the ground.   (If you are a lefty you can reverse the hands on this step.)

Mumbley Peg is neither as difficult nor as dangerous as it may sound, as there is logic to every challenge.   By the time I was 12 I could make all 15 challenges without a miss about 80 percent of the time.

Choir Practice

My mother was not religious but she was very friendly with a stout Episcopalian, Mrs. Kaufman, who lived across the street. Mrs. Kaufman had three boys who sang in the choir at the Church of the Nativity.   Feeling that she was doing her motherly and civic duty, my mother agreed to send my brother and me to Sunday school and choir practice with the Kaufman kids.   Each Sunday we trudged across the bridge to the church on the other side of the river with the Kaufmans.   Sunday school wasn't so bad, possibly even interesting, but choir practice was horrible.   All those big guys with long white robes singing from a hymn book, and I didn't have a clue how they knew what notes to sing.

After two weeks my brother and I decided to play hooky and hung out on the bridge waiting for the Kaufmans to come out so that we could walk home with them. Mimi must have gotten the word, but she never pressed the issue. Perhaps something rubbed off on me, as I basically follow the golden rule – but I can scarcely claim to be a pillar of the church.

Harvey Sterner and the Putz

Anybody who lived in Bethlehem knew what a *Putz* was, but surprisingly, nobody else in the country ever heard of it, at least that is what I found out later. In any case, a kid named Harvey Sterner lived across the street from me on Hanover Street. Harvey was clever at building things, and he had the greatest *Putz* I had ever seen – railroad trains running around mountains and through tunnels, with lakes made out of mirrors, and the Manger scene – all on a big table in his house. We spent a lot of time helping Harvey build new features for his *Putz* . I never did find out where the word *Putz* came from, but it must have been of Pennsylvania Dutch derivation.

Harvey was a natural leader and sometimes a bunch of us kids would hang out at his house when his parents were not home and have fun with the telephone. For example, we would call up the local grocer and ask him whether he had Prince Albert in a can   (that was pipe tobacco in those days). When the grocer said "Yes, we do," Harvey would retort loudly, "Well, let him out!" Pretty corny by today's standards, but we found it highly amusing in those simpler days. It helped that nobody could tell where you were calling from, like they can today.

Harvey was handy at other things too. He once built a row boat in his basement – a real nice job. The only problem was that he miscalculated the size of the basement door and it wouldn't fit through. It just proved that even the cleverest kid could have an Achilles heel. What was Harvey's solution? He ripped out the doorframe and squeezed it out.

My Pater and the Royal Tap

My father was kind of a unique guy. Trained in his early life as a ship draftsman, he was hired by the Bethlehem Steel Company and worked first in the steel company's Sparrows Point Shipyard in Maryland, then came to Bethlehem, where he was converted to an Estimator, whose function was to calculate the specifications for the steel required for specific jobs, including the configuration, size, quantities, tonnage, etc.

Dad was a fairly small man who dressed and acted like an English gentleman; i.e., he always carried an umbrella and always stood up and offered his seat to a lady on the trolley car or bus.

I don't know where he acquired his style, as he was born and raised in Harrisburg and Philadelphia. However, the surname of his mother (my grandmother) was Montgomery, and he claimed he could trace his ancestry back through the Montgomerys in England, as well as the Montgoumereys, who arrived from

France, I think, with the Norman Conquest or some such. Didn't we all?

Anyway, Dad used to relate various bits of history and tell me stories about this and that. In doing this, he had a strange habit of cuffing me lightly (affectionately) on the back of the head, with an upward movement, and saying, "Don't you know, Eddie?" Harvey Sterner found this highly amusing and soon dubbed it, "The Royal Tap." Harvey would give me a cute little upward cuff on the back of my head and proclaim grandly, "The Royal Tap, and up de back!

I wonder what ever happened to Harvey Sterner – a mischievous and clever kid, and also a good soul. I hope he had a good life. He deserved it.

Chapter Three

GOLDEN GATE CONTRACT – SOME RELIEF FOR THE STEEL COMPANY

1932 - 1934

Helping Plan the Bid

Although the layoffs and cutbacks in working time continued during the early years of the thirties, my own family was more fortunate than some of the men in the shops.   While my father was not a high paid executive, the main office staff had to perform all of the functions and calculations to keep things running.

There was one short period of time during which the office staff was cut back to 3 days per week,   However, by early 1932 it was well known that bids would be accepted later in the year for a company to build the planned Golden Gate Bridge across San Francisco Bay. Bethlehem Steel was eager to win that great plum, as it desperately needed the work. As discussed above, Dad's job was to compute and estimate the types, specifications, and quantities of the steel that would be required for the bridge, and he was deeply involved in the calculations and planning for the bid.

As it turned out, Bethlehem Steel actually did win the bid for the bridge in November 1932. The contract was for approximately $11 million, which resulted in the delivery of 67,908 tons of structural steel over the next several years. The entire cost of  the Golden Gate Bridge was about $24 million, which sounds unbelievably cheap by today's standards.

As it turned out, however, the structural steel for the bridge was actually produced by McClintic-Marshall, a subsidiary of Bethlehem Steel, in Pottstown, Pa., and was shipped via the Panama Canal. Therefore, it did not do much for the people in the Bethlehem Steel shops, but it kept the planning staff busy and helped the company's bottom line.

In the years that followed, Dad told me quite a bit about the construction of the bridge.   He was particularly concerned about the difficulties of sinking the great caissons which had to go down 235 feet below the surface of the water to support the massive weight of the bridge. That was quite a challenge and required a lot of dangerous work by the "sand hogs", who worked every day under high pneumatic pressure, like those who built the New York tunnels, risking serious injury or death from the "Bends." As I grew older I read a lot about the "sand hogs" and the jobs they do, and also developed a special interest in underwater salvage, which has similar perils.

Pembroke, Northeast Bethlehem

When I was 9 my family moved to the northeast section of Bethlehem, in an area called Pembroke. It was a decent neighborhood with friendly neighbors, but best of all was that we lived at the end of a street abutting countryside abundant with fields and trees.

The Hanged Man Tree, Field Fires, and other Adventures

On the day we moved in I went with a couple of other kids to the nearby field and saw a rope dangling from a limb of a big tree. We then heard that the day before a man had hanged himself there. I never found out why, but it was the Depression, nobody had any money, and I guess some people were having a really bad time.

The neighborhood was loaded with kids, but I was about the youngest in the pack. Consequently, I was the butt of a lot of tricks played by the older kids, including my brother, who was

12.   In the summer time, we had a lot of field fires around us, after the grass got good and dry.   One day somebody suggested lighting a small patch on fire to see how it burned.   I was pretty gullible in those days.   After the others seemed to be having trouble getting it to burn, I blurted, "Let me try."   Next thing I knew the field was blazing with flames 30 feet high that were spreading into adjoining fields.   Six fire engines came; we ran like hell and I hid in the house.   Nobody squealed.

Then there was the street light.   On the street corner near our house there was a high light fixture that had a bulb surrounded by a metal reflector shade.   One of the neighborhood kids had a BB gun, and they were taking turns trying to shoot out the bulb, but everyone was   (accidentally, of course) missing .   Once again the gullible kid (me) spoke up and said, "Let me try." Bing!   The first shot caused a big blue flash and the street turned dark.   Everybody scrambled – me first, with the kids yelling after me,   "The cops are going to nail you!"   I made myself scarce for a while and avoided jail again.

I had a strange experience in that place.   One day I was walking down the street with some kids.   We passed a tree where a big black hawk was sitting up in the top, making a strange sound.   I don't know why, but I announced, "I'm going to climb up and get that bird."   The kids said I was nuts and that he would fly, and of course they were right.   I climbed up the tree, getting closer and closer, but he didn't fly.   Finally, I reached out and grabbed him and brought him down   He had a broken wing.   I took him home and we put a splint on it.   He must have been starved because I actually got him to eat a bit.   After about a week he left, I don't know how, he just disappeared.   Was there something symbolic about that episode?

Economy Gardens

The Depression was deepening and the local government launched a program which encouraged people to plant gardens in fields that were apparently either owned by the city or provided by a few farmers who were not planting them. They were called "Economy Gardens." My married sister and her husband managed to get a half-acre of land near our house, and somebody provided a guy with a horse and plow to dig it up.

You would be amazed at how many vegetables you can grow on a half-acre, and how much backbreaking work is required to keep it watered, weeded, and cultivated. I know, because I was conscripted for a bunch of the work and learned how to plant potatoes, corn and other vegetables.

I think it is something that most modern kids don't have a clue about.   They just eat the stuff and never give a thought to where it comes from. I actually found it rewarding that all those delicious vegetables were flowing from the earth. Particularly fascinating to me

Roasted Fingerling Potatoes – A Really Tasty Treat!

were the thousands of tiny potatoes that are on the roots when you harvest the regular sized ones. For years I wondered why somebody didn't do something with those little spuds. Somebody finally did, and these days, when we see them in the markets they are called "fingerling potatoes" and cost a small fortune.

Saturday Matinees

Speaking of rewards, of which most of them were psychic, my allowance was 15 cents a week. It might seem pretty grubby today, but in those days, if you played your cards right, it could

do some good. For example, movie seats were a dime and you could go into the Saturday matinee and stay for virtually the whole afternoon. Usually, we would go to the Nile Theater on Broad Street. Typically, the matinee on Saturday comprised a newsreel, coming attractions, one or two cartoons, an exciting cliffhanger serial (always continued next week, when you found that the train really didn't crunch the hero after all) a cowboy picture, and the main picture. Not too bad for an afternoon's pleasure.

What about the other nickel? It was good for a soda, some penny candy, or even a hot dog after the show. That's right; all sodas and delicious hot dogs (with mustard and onions) were 5 cents in those days. Today they are a couple of bucks, and half of the time they are not even hot. The deal on sodas turned even better when Pepsi came out with its 12-ounce bottle. Pepsi even had a little radio jingle, which went:

Pepsi Cola hits the spot

Twelve full ounces, that's a lot

Twice as much for a nickel too

Pepsi Cola is the drink for you!

I'll bet the Coca Cola Board of Directors held a special meeting over that!

Sometimes the theaters would hold special promotions to entice people to part with a hard-earned dime. Once in a while they had dish day (a free plate, cup or bowl was handed out to each patron) and at other times a vaudeville act would perform during the intermission before the main picture. I saw plenty of good acts this way, including some great magicians. I think even Houdini appeared once (but it may have been Blackstone).

One Saturday they had vaudeville and were giving away eight free rabbits. I was standing in a crowd up in the balcony watching all the kids crowd up to the stage with their hands out when I felt a nudge in the back and an usher said, "Here, kid" and handed me a rabbit. I was dumbfounded then, but I think I was more dumbfounded in the months that followed, when I found out that keeping a rabbit involved a lot of cleaning out cages and finding good stuff for him to eat.

Not too long after that, the city put a 10 percent tax on theatre tickets, so the cost of our Saturday matinees soared to eleven cents. There were a lot of hard feelings about that among the local kids, and it destroyed the continuity of my allowance.

Three Ring Circuses

In Bethlehem there was a piece of ground just off what is the present-day Easton Avenue, near Stefko Boulevard. Once a year a couple of competing circuses would come to town and they would always be held in that field. As the site was pretty handy, the neighborhood kids and I would trudge over and take in the excitement. One of the most exciting things to watch was the erection of the big tents, using the elephants to pull up the poles.

It was an amazing performance and the circus crews were really skilled. They would lay out everything and drive in the stakes (three guys on a stake with hammers hitting sequentially like automatons), the mahouts would back up the elephants, and bingo, the big top would rise magically! It was a well-rehearsed, choreographed performance.

Sometimes, at ShowTime, we would sneak under the big tent and get in free. There were some circus guys who watched for stuff like that – I think they were called Roustabouts – and they usually spotted us trying to sneak in.

Sometimes, when they were packing customers in, we really got rousted, but once in a while (when things were a little slow) one of them somehow managed not to be able to catch us in time and we pulled it off. We were little kids and I guess circus people were pretty good human beings who understood kids. After all, it was Depression time.

After Barnum and Bailey came up with the "Three Ring Circus" every circus had to advertise that they were featuring "Three Rings,' even if the rings weren't so big.

In any case, one Saturday afternoon, after having successfully negotiated the "under the tent" admission, a couple of us kids were watching the performance when all of the sudden some ropes and canvas in one of the rings caught fire and started to flare up, probably from a short in an electrical cable. Fortunately, the fire was quickly put out, and the show went on uninterrupted. However, years later, when the disastrous circus fire took place in Hartford, CT, and many people died in the conflagration, I was reminded of that day when I was a kid sitting without parents in the Big Tent.

Speaking of circuses, there was a retired circus man in our neighborhood in Pembroke and each summer he organized a special circus for all of the kids and our parents. I think his name was Wright, but am not sure. I don't know what that man did with the circus, but he was a great organizer with a kind heart. He had a pretty good sized tent which he set up in his back yard, then recruited lots of the neighborhood kids to come in and learn to perform an "Act". We had clowns, jugglers, magicians, a fortune teller with a glass ball, and even a high-wire walker. The wire was about three feet high, about six feet long, and the performer was usually a girl, who used an umbrella to keep her balance while performing. Sometimes her balance wasn't so good.

Shortly before the show, Mr. Wright circulated flyers throughout the neighborhood that read something like this:

ANNOUNCING

WRIGHT'S FAMOUS THREE RING CIRCUS

Featuring

Ferocious Wild Animals

Clowns and Acrobats

Talented High Wire Walker

and

Other Special Acts

Watch for the Circus Parade Saturday at 1:00 PM

Followed by

The Big Show

Sure enough, on Saturday came the big Circus Parade with lots of "wild and ferocious animals" (mostly cats and dogs, with an occasional garter snake), all in cages on wagons pulled by kids, and sometimes by big dogs in harnesses. There were clowns and kids in costume and lots of balloons and plenty of color.

The parents would line the road to see it, and had a great time. One time we even had a donkey, fitted out with an elephant's trunk and big ears. He was a big hit.

It's possible that Mr. Wright had really been a Ringmaster, because when the circus performance opened, he would appear in full regalia, including leather boots , breeches, cutaway coat and top hat, and proceed to announce each of the grand acts in a stentorian voice with plenty of adjectives extolling the virtues and fame of the performers.   Thinking back on it, I am reminded very much of the Our Gang movie series, where the kids would do things like that.   However, *Wright's Famous Three Ring Circus* was definitely a cut above.

I think that modern society could use a lot more Mr. Wrights, who gave of themselves for their neighborhood, and fewer people who find reasons to complain about a little noise or violation of zoning laws, etc. He was a fine person, and I hope he found the rewards in life that he earned.

Drain Pipes and the Candy Factory

In the Pembroke area there were some large concrete drain pipes that went into culverts. They were around 6 feet in diameter, and every once in a while someone would get the bright idea to explore where they went. We would go into the pipes equipped with matches and a candle and walk for blocks. Usually there was a trickle of water (or something) at the bottom of the pipes, so we walked with a straddle step. The pipes sometimes had a strong smell of sewer gas and it is a wonder that we didn't drop dead or blow ourselves up – but we didn't. They say that God protects kids and drunks. Who knows?

One Sunday we were exploring the pipes and there was a steel ladder hanging down, and we could see a manhole cover at the top. Four of us went up the ladder, opened the cover and began looking around. Guess what? We were inside of a candy factory! The first thing we saw was what looked like a little cement mixer, except that it was shiny silver (probably stainless steel) and was half full of those chocolate things that you spread on top of cookies and cakes. We stuck our grimy paws in and scooped out handfuls of the stuff, which was delicious and seemed not to be affected by the grime.

Just then we heard a watchman coming and we all quickly scurried down the ladder and closed the manhole cover. It was a wonder we didn't get shot. I hope nobody got ptomaine poison from eating the chocolate stuff that was left in the mixer.

Years later, when I went to Liberty High School one of my classmates was a boy named Ira Born. He was the son of the owner of the "Just Born Candy Factory." I never mentioned our adventure to Ira.

Fifty years later I visited Bethlehem and the "Just Born" factory was still there, but greatly enlarged. Among other things, they make a lot of those little pink and yellow peeps that people put into Easter baskets. I guess Ira or his progeny own the place.

During the same visit, I had a tough time finding my old house, as everything had been built up. No more fields or hangman's trees.

Depression Beach

In the early 1930s one of the greatest places to swim in Bethlehem was the concrete dam on the Monocacy Creek, which we called "The Second Dam." To find the place today, you need to go to the bottom of Shoenersville Road where the railroad tracks cross the road, then walk up the tracks for about a quarter of a mile. There you will see the remains of the dam.

The water from the dam was backed up about a quarter of a mile, and at places where the water was deep there were a couple of diving boards. There was also an island at the upper end of the pond that was called "Duck Island."

On any hot weekend, hundreds of people would congregate there for swimming and family picnics. At some point someone opened a little refreshment stand and put up a sign that read, "Depression Beach." The name stuck, and soon there were few people in Bethlehem who did not know of Depression Beach.

Often the trains roared right by the dam and the engineers would blow the whistle just for fun. There were lots of little kids around but nobody ever got run over by the train. I guess kids were savvy about stuff like that in those days. I learned to swim at Depression Beach and remember it fondly.

The Red Men

There was a paint mill in back of the "Second Dam," at the intersection of the RR tracks and Shoenersville Road. The mill made red lead paint, and I believe the steel company was its biggest customer, as it was used to paint beams and girders. Sometimes we would see mill workers come out for a break or a smoke. We called them the "Red Men," as they were covered from head to toe with the deep red powder that they ground up to make the paint.

I suspect those poor guys are long gone, as that stuff is deadly. But it was Depression time, and there was no public outcry. Having a job and a paycheck came first!

Across the railroad tracks from the second dam was an area where clear water ran through a low grassy plain. If you knew where to look, some of the most delicious watercress grew there. I don't see it much in markets any more.

Blackmailed at 9

Another good place to swim was Illicks Mill, which we called the "Third Dam." Also on Monocracy Creek, it was farther upstream from the Second Dam and quite a bit deeper in places. My mother, who apparently had little confidence in my swimming ability, said she did not want me going there. Naturally, that increased the attraction and I sometimes joined a group of kids and trudged out there for the day.

I have heard that the place is quite different today, but back then the Third Dam was fairly decent sized and had a steady flow of water, about 2 inches deep, flowing over the top of it. As I recall, there was a fairly flat place on the dammed-up side, then a gradual slope to the spill edge, where there was a straight drop-off to the stream bed. Sometimes people would walk across the top of the dam, but carefully, as the water had created a slippery coating of moss and slimy weeds.

Once when I was there, some of my friends were on the other side, so in bare feet and a swimsuit I decided to walk across the dam. It was easy until I slipped. Next thing I knew, I was sliding down a slippery slope. There was no stopping and I sailed over the edge and dropped about 9 feet or so. There was a ton of rocks at the bottom and very little water, but as luck would have it I landed in the only sandy patch under the entire falls and scrambled ashore, a bit shaken but unhurt.

So much for that episode, except that my older brother heard about it from the other kids and, believe it or not, decided to blackmail me for my allowance! "I'm gonna squeal on ya to mom," he sneered, "unless you fork over your allowance [15 cents]." I should have called his bluff, as my mother was not severe and my father was a fairly soft touch. But my pride got in the way. My brother knew an easy mark when he saw one, so I paid up for two weeks straight, which put a crimp into my Saturday cowboy movies. The story finally oozed out anyway. I knew he couldn't keep his trap shut.

Quarantines

It is correct to say that during the 1930s, there were fewer restrictions on what you could and could not do. Dogs and kids roamed pretty freely and usually didn't get hassled except by other dogs and kids. The cops only stepped in if you pulled some outrageous stunt. However, not everything was freer than it is today. For example, you weren't free to spread your infectious diseases around to other people, as you can today.

I experienced the proof of that when I came down with a rash that turned out to be a case of the measles. My parents called a doctor, who didn't provide much treatment except Calomel

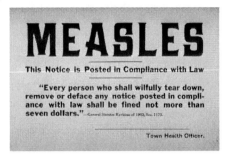

MEASLES

This Notice is Posted in Compliance with Law

"Every person who shall wilfully tear down, remove or deface any notice posted in compliance with law shall be fined not more than seven dollars." —General Statute Revision of 1902, Sec. 1173.

Town Health Officer.

pills (early-day aspirin), and ordering bed rest in a darkened room

However, a guy from the Department of Health promptly showed up and posted "Quarantine" signs all around the house. Nobody was allowed to enter the house and I believe that passers-by were warned to stay at least 25 feet away. I guess that is how we managed to beat some of the infamous epidemics. Now, of course, because some standards have been loosened in the name of preserving everyone's freedom, some of the old diseases are coming back.

Truants and Truant Officers

Another area where you weren't free to do whatever you pleased was going to school. Every kid under the age of 17, I believe, was required to go to school, unless the parents could prove absolutely that there was a need for that kid to stay home or go to work. There was no such thing as home schooling, and there was no such thing as passing a wiseass kid who goofed off and failed, just so the slob would not be embarrassed in front of his peers.

I don't know what ever happened to those common sense ideas, but they surely went away.

Don't misunderstand me; school was not a prison. They merely required minimum standards of behavior and did not let the kids take over the school. If you missed a day of school, your parents were required to provide a note explaining your absence. Of course, most of us kids played "hooky" once in a while, which we finessed by faking a note from our parents (A little petty forgery).

However, you had to watch where you hung out because all of the towns had at least one guy who was called a Truant Officer, whose full time job was to go around looking for kids who were roaming around during school hours.

Those guys were actually cops of a sort, who wore an official badge and had the authority to round up truants. They were pretty smart about where to find the kids too, and would continually troll some of the favorite spots, such as good fishing holes in the local creeks.

My mother was really good about the whole situation and would actually let my brother and me skip a day once in a while if our marks were ok and we had something special going. She would simply write a note which read, "Please excuse the absence of Edward yesterday; he was indisposed."

She would hand me the note, laugh and say, "I am not telling any lie. You were indisposed - to go to school." Mimi was great!

Home Entertainment and Musical Beginnings

While we had radios, most people did not sit in front of them all day long. Kids listened to a few favorite radio programs such as Jack Armstrong, Little Orphan Annie, and Sky King, which would begin around five o'clock in the afternoon on school days.

On Sunday evenings our whole family would sit in on a couple of programs, which included a comedy hour as well as the Ford Symphony Hour, which was excellent and gave me an early appreciation of good music.

One time when we were at Depression Beach a guy had a guitar and was singing songs with a crowd around him. When I got home I announced to my parents that I would like to learn to play the guitar. My interest in music was noted with enthusiasm and I was promptly launched on a musical education – but with a slight twist. My father would have gone along with the guitar, but my mother, who was a devotee of classical music, skewed things around a bit and signed me up for music lessons – on the violin!

I don't think Mimi ever heard of classical guitar, and that was before the days of the great Andrés Segovia and his superb suites of music for "guitar and orchestra."

I was naive, of course, and figured that if it had strings the violin could be OK. Boy, did I have a lot to learn. In any case, for the next nine years I trudged over to my music teacher for a violin lesson every Saturday. More on this later.

Duesenbergs – Cheap!

I had a married sister who lived in Fountain Hill, a suburban section of Bethlehem which ran along the base of South Mountain. At times when my family visited her, my brother and I would spend a goodly amount of time roaming around the area.

1934 Duesenberg   **Artist John J Purdy**

One day the two of us were walking down the main street and stopped to look at two cars that were sitting side by side in a Used Car lot. They were giant limousines in very good shape, and both of them were beautiful Duesenbergs. The hood of one was open and I remember counting the cylinders in the long powerful engine. Both were for sale – but not a customer in sight, anywhere. The asking price? $75 for one, $65 for the other. The Depression was real. Today, any Duesenberg is worth over a million dollars.

Moonshiners

Sometimes, my bother Bob and I would roam up into the woods that covered the mountainside above Fountain hill. They were pretty thick, and we once came upon a fully operating bootlegger still with kettles of mash steaming away and not a soul in sight. The bootleggers were probably watching us from the woods and I guess we were lucky not to get a kick in the rear or worse.

The "Revenuers" must eventually have gotten wind of what was going on in Fountain Hill, because a couple years later, while walking through those woods, we found lots of old copper tubes, kettles and tubs, all sliced up where the federal agents had liberally applied the ax to them.

North Carolina was apparently not the only place where moonshiners were plying their skills, but I guess the woods were deeper there.

Dance Marathons

About that time the dance marathon craze hit America. People would do virtually anything for a chance to win a few dollars and the dance marathon promoters exploited that desperation to the hilt.

They would hire a dance hall and some kind of cheap band, and sign up a group of couples, usually teenagers, for the Marathon. Sometimes they would hold one at the Central Park, and my sister would take us there to watch.

It was a cruel and hideous spectacle, where the idea was to see which couple could last the longest without falling down or dropping out.

The marathons went on for weeks and weeks, night and day. Of course, the couples were allowed to have specified minimum rest and refreshment periods but otherwise had to keep moving on the floor or be disqualified.

The result of this grind was that in the wee hours of the night or morning, they barely moved, with one partner sometimes sleeping while the other basically dragged the other fast enough to claim they were still dancing.

During the prime afternoons and evenings there were "rally" periods when a large audience would gather to urge on their favorites. Sometimes they would toss coins, like Romans urging on the gladiators who were about to die in the arena.

Then, the band stepped up the music and the radio announcer reported gleefully on the daily "fun."

My sister's best friend, Alice Robey, and her partner actually won a dance marathon after weeks of exhaustion, and collected the magnificent prize of $75. They went into the dressing room, fell asleep, and somebody stole the money.

Chapter Four

HEART OF THE DEPRESSION

1934 – 1936

Wydnor/Seidersville

In 1934, when I was 10, Mimi finally found a place which offered everything she sought, and my family moved to Wydnor, Pennsylvania, a suburb which was over South Mountain, about 8 miles from Bethlehem. That was one of the best things that ever happened to me. I went to school in a little four-room (eight grades) schoolhouse in Seidersville, where we had four months' vacation so that the farmer kids could help their parents on the farm. That was a win-win situation for us non-farm kids. (More on Seidersville School later.)

81

Wydnor was a paradise for kids. Our house was situated at the end of a cobblestone road about an eighth of a mile off the main road, and was surrounded by lovely fields, with a large woods and a stream about 500 feet away. My mother, who was a country lady at heart, loved everything about the place, as it was quiet, private, and surrounded by natural beauty in many varieties. A large meadow beside our house became a sea of wildflowers in the spring, and the entire field was covered in glorious buttercups and bluebells. I don't know what ever happened to all of the bluebells and buttercups in the countryside. Maybe the insecticides killed most of them off, because I have seldom seen them growing wild since then.

Later, that same field erupted with wild strawberries which, while tiny compared to cultivated ones, were absolutely unbeatable in taste. Early in the morning, my mother, who usually wore a large apron, would go into the field carrying a dishpan. She would pick the berries and put them into her apron, then empty the apron periodically into the dishpan. Typically, in a couple of hours she would pick half a dishpan full!

Over and above the wild berries , Mimi also had her own garden, which she gloried in. Actually, it was almost a half acre and might have been considered a small truck garden. I thought I had learned a lot about gardening from my sister's Economy Garden, but Mimi's garden took me into a whole new dimension. Over and above the regular stuff, like corn, potatoes and tomatoes , she grew watermelons , squash, lettuce , beets, cabbage, sweet peas, turnips, lima beans, spinach and celery. Maybe I missed a few.

She also grew some "old fashioned stuff" like kohlrabi (a type of cabbage) and rutabaga (like a yellow turnip) as well as parsley and basil for garnish. Also standing out in my memory were a patch of rhubarb, for making rhubarb pies, and a fair sized patch of eggplant. I could never understand what she saw in the eggplant, and when I asked she said my father really liked it when she made Welsh Rabbit. That shocked me, as I could not imagine my kindly mother knocking off the poor bunnies that were trying to catch a snack in her garden. She laughed and said that it was a dish she made by frying sliced eggplant with cheese and other stuff on it. I still don't understand where the rabbit came from.

It was certainly a lot of vegetables and I decided that the farmers called them truck gardens because it would have taken a truck to cart all the stuff away. I was frequently drafted to help with the weeding and cultivating, but, curiously enough, I don't recall ever seeing my older brother working the garden. That guy was real slick about being occupied somewhere else when that task came along.

No Shoes or Shirts in Paradise

There was a great bunch of kids in Wydnor and we all had one thing in common. Other than at school, no one except sissies wore shoes or shirts, and a simple pair of shorts was definitely de rigueur – as well as easy on the laundry requirements. However, there was a necessary period of toughening the foot soles to withstand the punishment. It usually took several weeks or so of "ouching" until we reached the proper thickness.

The supreme test of having made it over the hurdle was the ability to run on cobblestones and on freshly cut alfalfa stalks without punching holes in our soles. Those stalks can be very tough and sharp.

There was an excellent patch of woods near our house and I spent a great deal of my time roaming in them. By early summer I was not only brown as a berry and might have passed for an Indian, but I liked to practice being one. There were some paths through the woods that I knew well and I would trot along trying to be as silent as possible and not to disturb any foliage to leave a trail by which my enemies could track me. They never did, but you would be amazed at how many interesting things you could come across when you move silently thru a forest environment. I would surprise all kinds of animals, including deer, rabbits, possums, skunks, raccoons, and occasionally a snake sunning himself on a rock. I never saw a bear, but I think there were a few around.

At the edge of the forest there was a good sized section which was thickly covered by vines, where I found a nice little natural house made out of vines, and that became my special secret place.

Amazingly, in the springtime there was actually a small natural spring right in floor of my house where I could get a nice cold drink of water. At the beginning of the season it began as a tiny seepage, but I would make a point of clearing it out until I had a pool about 18 inches across and 5 inches deep, with a steady flow of water. Interestingly, the flow of water contained tiny golden flakes which would flicker in the sunlight which showed through an opening in the vines. At first I thought they were really gold, but of course I soon found out that they were mica.

A dandy stream ran through these woods, filled with minnows and some fair-sized fish. I didn't fish there much, but I knew where all of the interesting pools were. Another thing that it had was lots of frogs. I observed them growing from tiny tadpoles into frogs and some of them became quite large. In fact, I became a real expert at catching frogs by quietly sneaking up on them when they were sitting there, and anticipating where they would jump.

Did you know that you can hypnotize a frog? Absolutely. All you have to do it turn him over and gently rub his belly with your finger. I think it puffs him up or something, because you can then set him down again and he will not move. You can pick him up as many times as you want. Try it.

'Pop Pop' Boats

I also had a lot of fun with little "Pop Pop" boats, which I would sail in one of the quiet pools I created by clearing out rocks. They were the grandest little boats I ever saw. About four inches long, they were little all metal cabin cruisers, made in Japan, and cost a dime. Why did they call them "Pop Pop" boats? Believe it or not, they actually had a tiny flat boiler in the roof of the cabin, with a little pipe that led to the back as an underwater exhaust (and intake) pipe. A small candle sat in the middle of the boat, and when you lit the candle it caused the little boiler to first draw in a tiny amount of water, then heat it to point where it made a pop and expelled the hot water, after which the process kept repeating and the boat propelled itself neatly while making a continuous "pop pop" sound.

As long as the candle burned the boat would keep popping. When I ran out of candles I found that I could bring a small bottle of kerosene (we called it coal oil) and some old rags. I would stuff some rags into the boat, pour a little kerosene in and light it. Flames would came out of the portholes and I was at first afraid that it would melt the solder, but it didn't. Those things would run for about ten minutes at a crack.

I wonder what ever happened to "Pop Pop" boats, as I have never seen any since. Probably at some point the authorities decided they were dangerous and banned them. Or maybe after Pearl Harbor, which came along some years later, they decided that they were another fiendish invention of the enemy. Maybe they were, but they gave me an early appreciation of Japanese marine engineering and technology!

Dam Building

There was a spot in Wydnor where the creek was a little wider, so every spring the local kids would build a dam there for swimming. There was a grass-covered field not too far from there where we could dig sod as our principal dam-building material.

Basically, the dam would be anchored by a few large boulders, and sometimes a log or two, and then built up with sod. A couple of bigger kids would be designated the dam builders, two more would dig sod, and the rest of us would line up like Egyptian slaves, fill our arms with sod, and slog it down to the dam site.

It took about a day to create a true dam, but by late afternoon we had water rising in the dam to a depth of 4-5 feet, not bad for a cold dip, and very close to home. Speaking of cold, we would start those dams in April. Can you imagine how cold creek water is in April? That first dip felt like diving into ice water, but kids are resilient and we quickly became used to the cold water.

Our dams were so efficient that sometimes we would end up virtually shutting off the stream below the dam. A number of farms depended on that flow to provide water for their cows, so every once in a while one of the farm kids would walk upstream, locate the dam, and break down a piece. There were no hard feelings and everybody understood. We would simply build it back up again, and sometimes open it up for a while to keep some water running downstream.

Most of our serious swimming, however, took place in the nearby mine holes, which were former open-pit zinc mines that filled up with water when a certain depth was reached and underground rivers were tapped. (More on this below.)

Fire in the Theater

One Saturday when I was 10, my parents decided to drive into Bethlehem and do some shopping on the south side of town, and invited me to join them. Third Street, near the steel plant, is a virtual ghost town today, but in those days it was a burgeoning shopping district with a large fresh food market and stores of every variety. There was even a theater, which I believe was named the "Lyric."

Knowing that my parents would be shopping for several hours, I asked if I could go to the movie, and they said, "Fine, we'll meet you at the car later."

I remember that the movie was an epic about the winning of the West, called The Big Trail. Of course, it was in black and white, as all movies were then, and I recall that just at the point where the covered wagons were being lowered over the cliff into the valley below, the screen started to turn pink. That's odd, I thought, assuming it must be some kind of new color process, but suddenly the pink turned red and the entire screen burst into flames!

I have since read about many theater fires that had disastrous consequences, but oddly enough, there was absolutely no panic in that theater. Everyone just stood up and made their way to the door with no problems. Nobody even offered me a hand. I simply walked out with the rest. The theater was not crowded, and that probably helped.

However, thinking back on it, I am amazed that the theater was not required to have fireproof screens and curtains. If there were laws dictating that it was, that theater was in violation. In any case, the point was moot as nobody was hurt, and the theater was so severely damaged that it disappeared from the scene forever.

Halloween

Halloween was a pretty special time in the country. There was no such thing as "Trick or Treat;" it was all trick, and the kids had some pretty creative ideas, such as putting a family's Maytag washing machine up in a tree, then later going back and bringing it back down without a scratch. (Washing machines were smaller and had more places to grab onto then, instead of the square blobs that they are today.) I never even heard of Trick or Treat until we moved into the city, and frankly, after Seidersville/Wydnor, I thought it was a wimpy business.

We almost got into big trouble one Halloween. Kids often stretched toilet paper across the road and watched cars slam on the brakes at the last minute. That was ok, until some stupid kid decided to stretch a rope across. Nobody had ever seen a motorcycle cop in Wydnor before, but believe it or not, that was the night that one came along! Fortunately, he was not injured, but everybody took off like a shot, and a short time later there were cops running all around the place with flashlights, asking questions. One came to my house and inquired. I wasn't home, but I overheard it all, as I was hiding underneath the front porch, sweating bullets.

One of the good things about Halloween was that we usually ended up building a nice fire in some field, and having a feast. Sometimes the kids called it a "Steal", and that may have been technically correct, but it really wasn't grand larceny. The fact is that kids could have a great feeding bash right off the land; the only ingredient you needed from the house was some salt.

There were always potatoes, which we would cover in mud and toss into the fire. When they emerged, baked, you would simply break them open and add a little salt for a delicious snack. Other readily available foods were carrots, corn on the cob (wet the husks down and toss into the fire) and for desert some great roasted apples or other types of fruit. Nobody ever even thought that we needed a bag of chips or anything. Living off the land was easy.

Bareass Beach

In 1935 we were in the heart of the Depression, but none of us ever thought about it that way. We were lucky kids, living in a great area where we had lots of freedom and endless things to do. As I mentioned earlier, we got over four months of vacation from our little four-room country school, and that made for some great summers. For transportation, everyone rode bikes (magnificent one-speeders, what else), and we were on them morning, noon and night.

Most mornings, a kid named Jack Wray would ride down to my house at about 0900 and yell "Yo Eddie!" (He later went to Annapolis and became a naval officer.) Naturally I would zip out in shorts and sneakers, sometimes without a face wash or tooth brushing I was a good kid, but I never asked permission; my father was at work and my mother (Mimi) was laissez faire about my comings and goings. Never thinking to grab a drink or a sandwich, we would head a couple of miles south to the mine hole, our main summertime swimming hangout. A former zinc mine, it was 175 feet deep and sinister looking, with sharp rocks, steep banks and some real great jumps.

There were about nine of those mine holes in the countryside around Friedensville, all of them former open-pit zinc mines that filled up with water as soon as a certain depth was reached. They were great places to swim because the water came from underground springs, pure and clear. Actually, doctors recommended swimming in the mine holes, as the zinc in the water was considered beneficial for rashes, cuts and burns.

Typically, we would head for the big deep one, which we simply called the mine hole but was otherwise known far and wide as "Bareass Beach." That's right; what distinguished it from all of the others was that the big mine hole was for guys only – no swimming suits and no families. Therefore, everybody ran around with everything hanging out, no sweat. Actually, some girls did swim there with guys on summer nights. However, the water level was deep in the pit, and damned dark, so if you were a wimp or a lousy swimmer you never swam there.

Other nearby mine holes had unique names and applications. Lake Thomas actually looked like a good-sized lake, with low grassy banks, and cottages, as well as some diving boards. People lived there and it was a popular picnic and camping spot. Others that come to mind were called "Sandy Beach" (family swimming) and "Rocky" (deep, with steep rock sides and very uninviting), etc. They were a godsend to people who had little money (almost everybody), and nobody posted "No

Trespassing" signs or called the cops. Also, nobody sued, even when someone drowned.

The big zinc mine operated until the late 19th century, and for a while after it began to fill up with water some serious efforts were made to pump it. In fact, at one time the largest steam  pump in the world, imported from England, had been employed there. You could still see a deep shaft and a building where the pump had been embedded. The remains of the building were still standing, with two tall chimneys, all stone, and a couple of windows, giving the overall appearance of a large rabbit with two big ears, eyes and nose.

All day long we would hang out at the mine hole, lying in the sun on the rocks and occasionally engaging in various challenges. There were white limestones strewn around the rocks near the edge of the water, and one game was to throw a white stone in, wait a couple of seconds, and then dive down after it. You chased the rock down, with the water going from clear to light green to darker and then to a scary dark green, with the pressure building up in your ears. We were lean and skinny kids who could go all day without a nip to eat. However, getting a drink of water was not a problem, as we would simply dive down 8 or 10 feet, grab a mouthful of nice clean water, and head back up. We would ride home about five thirty – tan, tired and hungry. The end of a perfect day.

High Jumps

As we grew older we became a little more daring. There were some towering rocks at the mine hole, made of a material that looked like lava. It was a tricky climb up to a perch over the water, and we would make our way up there and sit looking out over the water. The rocks were about 60-65 feet high and a few of the bigger guys would jump from them, while an occasional hotshot did a swan dive. What made it tricky was that there were some big rocks down below which you had to clear to get to the water. Today, I am reminded of the cliff divers of Acapulco, but in those days we had never heard of them and television was many years away.

One day a couple of us decided to see if we could get up enough nerve to "jump it." Four of us sat around for about 20 minutes working up our guts. What was a bit disconcerting was that a guy had slipped on the jump rock not long before, and you could still see the dark splotches on the rock where he hit. Anyway, we eventually hit the "I will if you will" stage and damned if one kid didn't just take a leap and sail off.

"Oh, hell, we're in for it now," I thought, and took a leap of my own. I wasn't the first, but I was the second, and everybody had a couple of jumps that day. It was quite a drop and we found that we could count to 13 on the way down. Clearing the rocks turned out to be not so bad, but you still had to be careful not to slip on the takeoff.

The Friedensville Zinc Mine

Without swimsuits, we learned in a hurry to keep our legs together. One time I had them about a foot apart and it was like whips cracking me in the you know what. Also, without a suit, a certain amount of water could get rammed up your posterior if you landed at a certain angle. That was my first experience with a natural enema.

1995 – Sixty years later, I am in Bethlehem and decide to visit the old mine hole to see what it looks like. I drive out the old black-tar pike to Colesville near the site and guess what; the road has been completely blocked off. Nobody knows anything about the mine hole. Using another route, I drive around to the Friedensville church, which looks just as it did 60 years before. I know that there is a small mine hole behind the church and that Bareass Beach is about one-eighth of a mile up the road. When I arrive I can hardly believe it; they are all gone! Vanished forever! No mine holes, just a great big business park with buildings and paved streets.

To exploit the abundant supply of zinc ore in the Saucon Valley, Samuel Wetherill organized the Pennsylvania and Lehigh Zinc Company in 1853. Built on the banks of the Lehigh River just south of Bethlehem. Wetherill's zinc plant remained in operation until 1911. When Lehigh University opened in 1866, the first chemistry professor was Charles Meyer Wetherill, Samuel's first cousin. As with so many other industries, little now remains of a once-flourishing business.

Source: Library of Congress and Pennsylvania Historical Association

What Took Place

In 1947, a zinc company launched an ambitious plan to restart the mines. The idea was to sink a deep shaft and shoot grout into all of the underground streams to clog them up and shut off the flow. I know, because after World War II, my friend Frank Rice (ex-combat Marine) and I actually spent about six months working on drilling rigs that were employed digging a deep shaft, which was to be enclosed in a concrete collar. Every day, trailer truckloads of dry cement arrived and this was mixed with water into a slurry called grout and shot down the drill holes to fill up the underground streams.

I was recalled to active military service shortly after that, and didn't find out until many years later what had happened. The underground streams had been shut off all right, and in the process everybody's wells for miles around were destroyed. The zinc company ended up offering to install metal cisterns for all of the country people whose wells had dried up – not a very sanguine solution for people who had been used to drinking pure spring water.

The net result was also a drying out of all the mine holes, but apparently the whole deal was a flop anyway and, from what I understand, they eventually used the old mine holes as dumps for Philadelphia's trash, and then paved them over. What a waste!

Seidersville School

When we moved to Wydnor I went into the fifth grade at the Seidersville School and spent the next four years there. It was, as I noted earlier, a four-room schoolhouse with eight grades

being taught by four teachers. How did that work? Each room had two grades, sitting on opposite sides of a big classroom with no divider wall. The fifth grade would study some lessons while the teacher taught the sixth grade for a half-hour, and then they switched roles. This meant that the fifth grade could also listen to everything being taught to the sixth graders, and vice versa. If you halfway paid attention, by the time you reached the sixth grade the lessons were a piece of cake.

We had double desks with inkwells, reminiscent of Tom Sawyer, where Tom would dip Becky Thatcher's pigtails in the well. In fifth grade I was assigned to sit beside a Pennsylvania Dutch farmer kid named Russell Wirth. Russ was a serious kid who believed in attending to his studies at all times and not whispering or doing anything disruptive. For a while he tended to be reserved, but after while he warmed up to me and we later became lifetime friends.

Seidersville School was great! Each of the four rooms had a furnace in the corner (the only heat in the school) and there was a big coal bin in the cellar. The big deal for the kids was when you got selected to go down in the cellar and fill up a coal scuttle. Curiously enough, the teacher always sent two kids, and of course they often managed to get lost down there for about 25 minutes, after which the teacher would send another kid to get them up.

Teachers were very imaginative in those days, and seemed to have lots of good ideas of their own. I believe they also had more freedom to improvise than teachers today, as there are a lot of standards to which modern teachers must comply. Anyway, my teacher for grades 5 and 6 was Mr. Wierbach, and he liked to experiment with new ideas. One day when we were studying geography, he posed the question of how we could remember the 10 largest states in the U.S., in descending order of their size. He suggested that each of us write a little ditty with the first letter of each state as the first letter for each of the words in our ditty. The states then (before Alaska was declared a state) in descending order of size were Texas, California, Montana, Nevada, Arizona, New Mexico, Colorado, Washington, Oregon, and Utah.

Many kids came up with verses like, "Tom's Cat Might Need a New Coat with-out Underwear." I don't know where it came from, but I wrote, "Together Came My New Attorneys; No Criminal Would Outwit Us." Mr. Wierbach was flabbergasted and read it out to the class, and all the kids turned around and stared at me. Mr. Wierbach's scheme worked, I guess, because I can still remember those states more than 60 years later. Of course, Alaska gets in the way now.

From that point on, everybody decided I was "a brain," but I did not care. I liked to read books, and went to the Bethlehem Public Library with my parents whenever possible. In fact all of my reading paid dividends, because I became a champion speller. Every few months the school had a spelling bee and one girl and I usually duked it out each time, alternating as champions. Mr. Wierbach had a way of grading everyone's "spelling age," and announced to the school when I was about 11 that mine was 16 – which earned me some Wows!

Bethlehem Public Library 1935

Mr. Wierbach was a pretty good child psychiatrist but he wouldn't take a lot of guff. One day he took a thick wooden paddle and whacked the butt of a sneaky kid who was called Sippi. I never did find out what his name really was, but that was what he was called. The kid belonged to some kind of super religious family that worked their kids to death and never let them go out of the yard, except to go to school. The result of all that oppression was that the kid naturally grew up as a rebellious jerk who craved attention but was universally hated. He pulled a real nasty stunt in class that day and the teacher gave him a dose of child

99

psychology with a one inch thick board. Dr. Spoch would never have approved, but the little creep never pulled that stunt again.

Raising the Body from the Deep

One day we came to school and our teacher did not show up. A couple hours later it was announced that they had found his clothes and his car at the big mine hole. The assumption was that he had jumped in. The next day they had a substitute teacher, but most of us kids skipped school and went out to the mine hole to watch the State Cops trying to raise Mr. Wierbach's body from the deep.

We sat on the rocks and watched while they rowed around with a rowboat and occasionally lowered some sticks of dynamite into the water and set them off to try to bring up the body. I must have been really hipped on Tom Sawyer, because it reminded me of Tom and Huck Finn watching when they were trying to bring up Huck's father's body by firing cannons over the Mississippi.

The dynamite didn't work, but after a week they found his body. We never knew it before, but he had severe intestinal cancer - and decided to end his life sooner. Sometimes good guys get all the bad breaks.

Chapter Five

Continuing Activities in the Country

1936 - 1937

Seventh and Eighth Grades

When I entered seventh grade the class was moved into the room taught by Mr. Shock, whom we all called "Shockey" – but not to his face. He was a quiet, unassuming man without any of the outward signs that might stamp him as even a mediocre teacher – but he really was the finest teacher I ever had. In seventh and eighth grades Shockey walked back and forth in front of the class, quietly lecturing us on various subjects and opening our skulls enough to allow a little culture to seep in. Over and above the standard stuff, he introduced us to classic poetry, asking each of us to memorize certain poems and then calling upon each student to stand up and repeat them verbatim, beginning to end. To this day, I still recall some of the great lines from poems such as "Invictus" by William Henley.

Out of the night that covers me,

Black as the pit from pole to pole,

I thank whatever gods may be

For my unconquerable soul.

In the fell clutch of circumstance

I have not winced nor cried aloud

Under the bludgeoning of chance

My head is bloody, but unbowed.

There was also Walt Whitman's "Oh Captain, My Captain" (commiserating the loss of Abe Lincoln), and especially "If," by Rudyard Kipling

First Stanza:

If you can keep your head when all about you

Are losing theirs and blaming it on you;

If you can trust yourself when all men doubt you,

But make allowance for their doubting too:

If you can wait and not be tired by waiting,

Or, being lied about, don't deal in lies,

Or being hated don't give way to hating,

And yet don't look too good, nor talk too wise;

Last Stanza:

If you can talk with crowds and keep your virtue,

Or walk with Kings – nor lose the common touch,

If neither foes nor loving friends can hurt you,

If all men count with you, but none too much:

If you can fill the unforgiving minute

With sixty seconds' worth of distance run,

Yours is the Earth and everything that's in it,

And – which is more – you'll be a Man, my son!

That was profound and impressive stuff for eighth graders.

Stein's Candy Store

School wasn't all work and no play in Mr. Shock's classroom, however. A kid named Harry Stein sat in front of me. Harry was a born merchant who ran his own little candy store right in school. Each day at recess and lunch time, he popped open his desk top and there was a ready-made sign on the underside that read, STEIN'S CANDY STORE – NOW OPEN. That was a built-in convenience that everyone appreciated, and Mr. Shock had no criticism so long as the store closed on time. I'm certain Harry did well in life, but I never saw him again after eighth grade.

Secret Messages

From the time I was about 11 I was interested in codes and signaling. A couple of friends and I had learned Boy Scout signaling with two flags, and practiced wig-wagging. I also taught myself International (Morse) Code so that I could use it with semaphore signaling (one single flag that you waved on either side of your body, with dots and dashes on alternate sides), and also using code beepers and lights. By the time I was 13 I had become so proficient that I was able to listen to the radio amateurs on some frequencies of our home radio and copy down their messages. Later in life, when I became an Aviation Cadet, my knowledge of Morse code came in very handy: I took the test and was out of code class in one day.

Also popular at the time were Orphan Annie decoder pins, and the kids would use them in class at Seidersville School to send various coded messages. They were nifty little gadgets with a rotating wheel with letters and numbers in a circle on the face, plus an outer circle of letters and numbers. By locking in any code setting we had an automatic quick coder and decoder system that would allow us to send various coded messages, some that might not have been appreciated if deciphered by the wrong person. Shockey was good about stuff like that. He saw the messages being passed around, but rarely confiscated the decoders unless the kids were getting obnoxious.

Sometimes at noon time I would write mysterious messages on the blackboard in Morse code, such as:

NEBINGER, the name you will remember.

Or even better,

REGNIBEN (Nebinger spelled backwards)

In International Code: .-.　.　- -.　-.　..　-...　.　-.

　　　　　　　　R　　E　　G　　N　　I　　B　　E　　N

I sometimes saw Shockey studying them, but he never said a word. Maybe he knew code, or maybe he was the kind of teacher who appreciated kids that had some gumption.

Spear Wars and Crack the Whip

Recess and lunch hour were periods of frantic and downright dangerous activities at Seidersville. A favorite game we played behind the school was called "Crack the Whip." I once made the mistake of being the end kid of a string of 15. When the whip cracked I went sailing about 10 feet and really wrecked a shoulder. I became a lot smarter after that.

In back of the schoolyard there were great fields and a creek. A popular game was "Spear Wars" in which the kids took dried reeds that grew along the creek and made them into spears. They then divided into sides and the war consisted of groups of kids throwing sharp spears at each other with every ounce of energy they had. There were lots of stick wounds and cuts and some near misses with eyes, but oddly enough I never heard of a kid losing an eye. Nobody ever thought to wear goggles. We didn't have any and if we had it would have been considered "sissy".

During bad weather we stayed inside and there was a tremendous bike-riding session that went on in the school basement. There were two huge rooms with concrete floors and a large hallway in between them. Kids ripped around in circles frantically in each of the rooms and then would shoot dramatically across the passageway and into the other room, trusting to luck that somebody else did not pick that minute to go the other way. There were lots of head-on collisions. We didn't have a school nurse, but the two lower grade lady teachers were pretty good with the iodine.

The standard bike in those days had 26-inch wheels and balloon tires (a one-speeder!). One Christmas, the parents of my friend Russell got him a new bike. Being old-fashioned, they bought him a skinny-tired 28-inch bike that looked very high and was most definitely not the popular design of the day. Was Russ concerned? Not at all; he simply called it his "Stagecoach." Kids are great at adaptation.

Hunting season was always an interesting time, as there were hunters looking for pheasants right behind the school. Every once in a while we would hear a bang and all of the kids would stand up on their seats to look out the back window.

Good old Shockey would simply ask, "Did he get him?" then quietly tell the kids to sit down. Imagine hunting 100 feet from a school building today!

Christmas at Seidersville School

Christmas was a special time at Seidersville School. On the morning of the day before the school let out for Christmas, all of the kids from the whole school filed into the 7th/8th grade room and stood against the wall three rows deep. One of the teachers played the piano, another one sang, and the whole school sang the old favorite Christmas Carols. It was a memorable time and everybody loved it. We might not have had God in our hearts, but we had Him in our school. In those days we didn't have any radical social agitators threatening to take the school to court for celebrating Christmas. There might have been some, but they kept their mouths shut.

Seidersville School is still there but has been closed up tight for many years. On the rare occasions when I visit Bethlehem these days, I drive by the school and wonder if the old double desks and coal stoves are still there. I also wonder if anyone else is left who shares those precious memories.

Flexible Flyers

Winter time was actually a fun time in Seidersville/Wydnor. Before they built the new Interstate 378 going down the south side of South Mountain, there was just the Old Philadelphia

Pike, a two-lane black top road which ran down through Wydnor. In those days they didn't bring out the snow plows every time it snowed. People with cars simply put on a set of tire chains and chugged up over the snow covered hills. South Mountain was pretty steep and on nights when there was a good coating of snow on the road there was quite a sledding party that took place on the Seidersville side. We would walk all the way up the hill, dragging our sleds behind, then fly down the highway at great speed, zip around the bend at the bottom of the hill, and cruise all the way to the bridge in Wydnor, a total distance of just over one mile (I measured it recently).

There weren't many cars on the roads in those days, but there were some and it is a wonder that none of us were killed, as we would fly through the crossroads on the side of the hill at about 50 miles an hour, without lights, and hope that a car didn't decide to cross at that time. For those who know Bethlehem, I am talking about the crossing on the side of Seidersville Hill where the popular Greek restaurant called "Yianni's Taverna" is now located. Recently, I sat in "Yianni's and thought about those days.

There was actually a pecking order in sleds, which was pretty important. Everybody knew that the Cadillac of sleds was the Flexible Flyer, which had its own unique insignia on the top.

We called them "Flexies," and they were absolutely better than other sleds because they steered really well and also seemed to go faster. I never owned a "Flexie, "but settled for some other brand which worked well enough. To place this into perspective, I guess I was just driving a Chevy instead of a Caddy.

Sometimes one of the local teen agers who had a Model A Ford would tow a bunch of sleds and sledders all the way back up to the top of the hill. I recall one time when a guy named Elwood Werner (Ellie), our neighbor in Wydnor, found a nice one-horse sleigh at some country auction and actually secured it to the back of his Model A by fastening the two shafts, one on each side of the car. A bunch of us kids went for a couple of miles crazy ride in that sleigh.

Sometimes, when Ellie found a wide spot in the road he would actually spin the car around with sleigh attached. When I think what the cops would do if they caught people doing stuff like that today it boggles my mind! But you know what; they were good days, not so many cars, not so many laws and cops to enforce them - definitely more freedom.

Riding Backwards

Our bikes were our cars and we went anywhere and everywhere on them, so that our legs became like steel. One summer day we were out at the mine hole and were clowning around on some large mounds which were left over from the old zinc mining days. They were quite a challenge for ripping up and down and we made a few jumps where we had a lot of fun but also managed to crash a few times, gouging our hands and arms on the cinders.

On that particular day we decided to try something new – sitting on the handlebars and riding backwards with our feet on the pedals. At first it seemed impossible, as we would instinctively want to turn the wrong way, but after a few crashes and some persistence we began to get the hang of it.

Artist: John J Purdy

At the end of that day all of us rode all the way home on the highway sitting on the handlebars and peddling backwards. It wasn't so tough after all and we had acquired a skill that would come in handy over the next few years – if we got a flat in the rear tire we could ride backwards, keeping the weight off that wheel until we reached a gas station where we could fix it and pump it back up.

Many years later I noted that Paul Newman had acquired the same skill, which he demonstrated in the movie Butch Cassidy and the Sundance Kid. I wonder if Newman had a great place like the mine hole to practice his handlebar skills.

The Pennsylvania Dutch and their Work Ethic

Almost all of the farmers in the Lehigh Valley were so-called Pennsylvania Dutch. Actually, the name is misleading as they were not Dutch but Deutsch (or German), and most of them spoke what was called Platt Deutsch, a form of low German. They were hard-working, God-fearing folks, firm in their work ethic but good, kind people and rock solid Americans. They also had a funny way of talking. For example, they might say, "Throw the horse, over the fence, some hay."

I was not a farm kid, but many of my friends were. They had assigned chores they had to attend to every day before they could go play with the other kids. Chores could include milking a specified number of cows, cleaning out stables, bringing animals in from the fields, feeding chickens or pigs, or a hundred other tasks. Sometimes I helped out, but by and large they did not expect help.

Their parents were always kind to me and understood that while I was not a "city kid," I was also not a farm kid. I simply made it a point not to drop by the farm kids' houses when they had chores to do. If I did get there early, I waited patiently for them to finish and were given the OK to go play.

I mentioned my friend Russell Wirth, who sat beside me in our double desk in the fifth grade at Seidersville School. Russ and I spent many hours wrestling and rough housing, and we would play hardy games of tackle football in the meadow with a bunch of farm boys – and their sisters.

I recall one time some years later (when I was almost 17) and showed up at the Wirth farm carrying a gas- powered model airplane that I had built. I was surprised to get a lecture from Russell, with a Biblical quotation tossed in, as follows:

"When I was a child I spoke as a child, I understood as a child, I thought as a child; but when I became a man I put away childish things."

Wow! Still water runs deep. I got the point. In Russell's mind a gulf had been crossed – childhood was behind us.

Spontaneous Combustion: Pulling sheep out of blazing barn

One day I happened to be standing on our back porch looking out over the gently sloping valley from our elevated spot. Suddenly I saw a barn go," Whoosh", and the entire roof blew off in a pillar of flame and smoke!

That barn was about 1 ½ miles away but I knew exactly how to get there the fastest way. I jumped on my bike and was already half way there before the Se-Wy-Co* Siren went off, and I was the first person there after the farmer.

112

I helped him pull four panicked horses out of the barn, and he went back for another one, while I dragged two sheep out of a pen inside the barn. Unfortunately, their long wooly coats were already afire, and even though we were able to beat the fire out, the poor creatures were so badly burned that the farmer had to kill them on the spot.

There were several more barn fires that year and I learned a lot about spontaneous combustion. One thing that was a definite "no no" was putting wet or even damp hay into a hayloft. You would think that the water in the hay would help keep it cool, but it works in just the opposite way. Apparently, as the temperature in the loft rises, those millions of bacteria in the damp hay start agitating at a faster and faster rate, raising the temperature of the hay at an exponential rate until the gases produced explode spontaneously with terrific force. Most city kids never learned about that.

The Ford Fire Engine. Courtesy Se-Wy-Co Fire Department

*Se-Wy-Co was the acronym for the local volunteer fire company. The name stood for Seidersville, Wydnor, and Colesville, the three communities it served. Se-W-Co had a single Model Ford fire truck,

113

and the local rumor had it that the truck was equipped with a governor.   I don't know if that was true or not, but I do know that I could beat it to fires on my bike, three times out of four.

Note: The reader may have taken note of the fact that fires of various types played a significant part in my early upbringing. I never had any desire to become a firefighter, but I learned to have a lot of respect for the job they do, and for the danger that fires can represent at an unexpected moment. In this regard, it taught me to look around carefully when I enter various types of structures, to locate the nearest exit and to think briefly of how I might evacuate my family.

When I had children of my own, I always set up a series of fire drills in our home, and devised various scenarios in which the kids had to play their parts. For example, if the bedrooms were on the second floor, I might announce, "The exit stairway is blocked by fire!" (They might be shown, for example, that there was an alternate exit, out the second story via the porch roof.) My children loved those drills; the older ones guided the younger, and everyone knew precisely how to handle various situations without panic. I highly recommend that parents think about home fire drills, where a small amount of effort can pay big dividends.

Eli Weaver and the Nazis

Because I was bitten by the airplane bug at an early age, it followed that I would become an avid reader of all things related to flying, including World War I aces, barnstorming, the

114

National Air Races and planes that competed in them, balloons and airships, and sailplanes. Further, at an very early age I also became a dedicated model airplane builder, a hobby that I retained well into adulthood, when I would sometimes travel hundreds of miles to compete in national contests.

My modeling activity ran the gamut from building solid-wood scale models to constructing rubber powered scale and endurance models, hand-launched and towline-launched gliders, and finally large competition-class free-flight gasoline engine-powered models. Radio control was in its infancy then, so I did not get to that until later in life. Once I even built a large scale model of a Zeppelin, about 36 inches long with lots of ribs and stingers and a tissue covering.

Model building required a bench where you could lay out structures while waiting for the glue to dry, but there was no available spot in my home, so in desperation I converted a big closet in my bedroom into my model shop. It was kind of a squeeze but I fixed things up real well and plastered the walls with pictures of airplanes and some of my aviation heroes. These included WWI aces Eddie Rickenbacker (U.S.), Frank Luke (U.S. balloon buster), Rene Fonck and Georges Guynemer (France), Billy Bishop (Canada), Baron Von Richthofen (Germany), Albert Ball (England), and Mickey Mannock (Ireland). There were lots of them, but these were among the top scorers.

I spent countless hours laboriously working on my airplane models, and on rainy days it was a perfect outlet for any free time that I had. That closet was lacking in ventilation, however, and often reeked with the fumes from the model cement and the airplane dope that we used for the coverings. Years later I was appalled to read about kids sniffing glue containing Toluol to get high, a very dangerous practice. I don't know whether the glue we used then contained any Toluol, but I doubt it, because if it had I don't think I would be writing about these memories today.

There were about a half dozen of us model builders in the Wydnor area, and Jack Wray, whom I have already mentioned in conjunction with our mine hole episodes, was one of them. Another model bug was a kid name Eli Weaver, and the three of us used to go fly our models together in one of the local fields.

Eli had a keen interest in the international news of the day and followed closely the events developing in Europe, as Hitler prepared his country for the conflict that would become World War II. Of course, none of us liked what was happening in Europe, but it was a long way away and didn't really impact us (then).

I don't know why, but for some reason Eli developed an absolute hatred for Hitler and the Nazis in every possible way. He was so passionate about it that the Wray kid found it to be almost comical, and made a point of coming up with sly cracks and jokes about the Nazis, just to get Eli's goat.

One time Jack Wray and I were visiting Eli at his house and he was showing us some of his models, which were really nicely made. Among his collection, Eli had a pretty nice biplane with about a twenty four inch wingspan. As a joke, when Eli was talking to me, Jack slyly painted some swastika insignias on the top wing of the biplane. Eli was a good sport and had a pretty good sense of humor, but when he turned around and saw those swastikas he got really mad, not at Jack, but at the Nazis in general, and launched into a tirade, at the end of which (to demonstrate his point) he jumped on that airplane and mashed it!

There is a supreme irony in that, and life surely moves in mysterious ways, as not too many years later Eli was destined to have a personal experience with the Nazis. In late 1943 he enlisted in the Army Air Corps and sought a flying job of some sort.

Eli was a rather small, wiry guy, and fitted nicely into the need for people of his stature to man the Tail Gunner position in bombers, where space was very limited. In 1944 he was Tail Gunner on a North American B-25 Mitchell twin-engine bomber assigned to the Fifteenth Air Force. They were on a bombing mission near the Brenner Pass in Italy, when the plane took a direct hit from a

The B-25D Medium Bomber
Source: U.S. Air Force

German 88 mm ack ack gun. (Eli told me this story after the war.) The wing folded and the plane headed straight down. There was a small escape panel in the tail gunner hatch and Eli was only half way through when he got stuck. In desperation he pulled his rip cord. The chute opened and dragged him out, badly injuring his right leg, but he landed safely.

Eli was captured and thrown into a temporary prison where he languished for three days without proper medical treatment. During this time he was visited by several members of the SS who peppered him with questions. It just so happened that Eli was carrying a small Bible with him, and that became a cause of great sport for the SS guys, who teased him about it unmercifully. Knowing Eli, I have no doubt that he told them what he thought of them.

On the fourth day, Eli was moved to an Italian hospital, where a German doctor examined his injuries, which had become very badly infected. Eli, who could speak Pennsylvania Dutch, understood enough German to overhear the doctor say that they would have to cut off the leg. He yelled loudly, "Nein, Nein, nicht schneiden! (Don't cut!)

The doctor came over to his bed and said, "You speak German?" Eli explained to him that he came from Pennsylvania, that his people were Pennsylvania Dutch, and that they spoke a German dialect (Platt Deutsch). That must have resounded favorably with the doctor, who actually saved the leg, but had to fuse the joint permanently.

Eli walked with one stiff leg for the rest of his life. Sadly, the war left other permanent but less visible scars that ultimately caused Eli to take his own life. Eli was the only member of his crew who survived the crash. He told me that his pilot, Captain Pickett, was a direct descendent of the heroic civil war General who led Pickett's Charge at Gettysburg.

Hitchhiking to Elmira at 12

My interest in model building and in airplanes also included Sailplanes, which were (and are) very sophisticated gliders which stay aloft for hours by riding thermals of hot air. In 1935 I was reading about the forthcoming National Soaring Society meet and competition to be held in Elmira, New York. The Wray kid and I got to talking about how we would really love to be at Elmira watching those sailplanes and a germ gradually crept into our heads, "Why don't we go and see it?" We checked a map and it was about 200 miles, which was a bit far for our bikes, but hitchhiking was popular then and did not have the bad name it has today, so we decided to give it a go.

Our parents had become accustomed to us being on our own in the summer, whether at the mine hole or at Boy Scout camp in the Pocono Mountains, so it was not so unusual for us to take off for a week. I don't know how Jack finessed it with his parents, but I casually mentioned to mine that we were planning to go to Elmira to the sailplane meet.

I don't think either of our parents knew where Elmira was and I guess they never bothered to check. In any case, each of us made up a little back pack that included a sleeping bag, half a pup tent, a tooth brush (believe it or not), an extra shirt and pair of shorts, and a few dollars – and off we went.

We actually made it to Elmira in one day and got a ride up to the top of Harris Hill, where we pitched our pup tent very close to where the main hangar for the sailplanes was located. It was a glorious place, overlooking a beautiful valley, and we were right at home in our element, close to nature. There were lots of magnificent gliders, including a couple from Germany. Jack and I discussed how our buddy, Eli Weaver, would not have liked that, as they were both proudly sporting swastikas on their wings!

We stayed almost a week, and had a great time. One thing that quickly became clear, however, was that we didn't bring nearly enough money, so that we were not exactly dining in style. What saved us, however, was that you could buy a good sized candy bar called a "Powerhouse Bar" for a nickel, and I think that for the last two days these comprised our principal diet. The profit margin on the "Powerhouse Bar" must have been pretty slim, because I haven't seen any since.

The trip back went pretty smoothly and we did not run into any major problems. There weren't a lot of sexual predators running around in those days, as their presence in society was not tolerated one iota. However, we were not dumb and knew about stuff like that.

Sure enough, we did get picked up by one kind of wimpy guy, who started right out asking questions like, "Do you boys like girls?" That was a clue and we just answered, "Nah – (we lied), we like boxing and fighting; we're going to try out for the Golden Gloves." There were no more questions and our journey back was uneventful.

I visited Elmira recently and went to the top of Harris Hill, much of which is now a park. It brought back poignant memories.

*National Soaring Meet, 1935, Elmira, New York. By John J.
Purdy*

Wild West Battles – for Real

One of the favorite games the local country kids played was
"Cowboys and Indians" or maybe more practically speaking,
"Range Wars", as you didn't want kids shooting arrows at each
other.   Basically, we made up teams and went around hunting
each other. They used to sell rolls of caps that you could put
into your cap pistol and they made a nice bang when you fired.
You would then yell out proudly, "I got ya, you're dead!"
Those caps would sometimes make sparks which could fly into
your eyes, so I guess they are illegal now, as I haven't seen any

for years. I know the game doesn't sound too appealing to modern parents, either, as the idea of simulating shooting somebody is definitely discouraged today, except in real wars, when it is OK. In fact, they give you a medal for that – if you're good enough at it.

Sorry, I digress. Anyway, when I was 12 I had a friend named Neil Gieske, who lived about a mile away. Neil, who was eleven, liked to drop by my place, so we could roam around in the nearby woods and creeks together. One Sunday, when he and some other kids were there, we decided to have a Wild West game, and my brother, Bob, who was 15, decided to join in. Bob didn't' have a cap pistol but he did have a .22 cal rifle which he used to plunk at various targets. If you guess what is coming at this point, your guess would be correct!

Now, you wouldn't think that anybody would be stupid enough to put real bullets into a gun while playing a game, but kids often fail to think out stuff like that. I guess that is why they need parents to keep them in line - but parents can't be everywhere. There we were, sneaking around, trying to nail one another, and in between our make-believe scenes, Bob was blithely taking pot shots at various targets of opportunity. Not people, of course, but – that's how accidents happen.

To make a long story shorter, he forgot he had a bullet in the gun and thought he would be just clicking on empty. Neil was hiding in a corner of our garage and Bob pointed the rifle around the corner and fired. There was a bang and Neil yelled, "Hey, you really shot me" and came running out holding his side. He was walking but blood was running out.

My father was not home, but we called my mother, who quickly came running out and took charge. She stripped off Neil's shirt and saw that the bullet had gone completely through, exiting in his back. Neil was having a little trouble breathing and we thought he might have a punctured lung. Mimi immediately put compresses on the wounds to stop the bleeding but it was a very serious situation and we needed to get him to a hospital immediately. My father was in town with our only running car, and no one with a car was nearby. To make things worse, while we had a phone, as luck would have it the line was down.

I jumped on my bike and rode as fast as I could to Neil's house where, fortunately, his father was home, and he immediately drove to our house, picked up his son, and we all made a frantic trip to the hospital. Miracle of miracles, the bullet had passed clean through Neil's body, narrowly missing his heart, lungs, and all vital organs!, but partly collapsing a lung – thus causing the breathing difficulty. Two weeks later, Neil was almost completely healed.

I shudder to think of the repercussions from this totally irresponsible act today. The lawyers would have a field day and ruin everyone's life. But that was 1936. Nobody had any hospital insurance; in fact nobody really had any money, so even if a lawyer had sued, it would have been a lost cause. In fact, my parents had been good friends of the Gieskes for years. There were profuse apologies, but there was never even a harsh word, and they remained close friends for the rest of their lives. My parents scraped up the money to pay the hospital bill, which was probably about 1/500th of what it would be today, and everybody moved on.

Needless to say, the .22 disappeared from the scene and was never seen again. I noted that when I got to be 15 nobody gave me a .22; I never even asked for one. My older brother, by the way, was the same one who accidentally burned the house down, a few years earlier. Older brothers can sometimes get in the way, by messing up everything before you can even get there!

Actually, I really didn't care, as I had a BB gun and became an absolute deadeye with the thing, being able to throw a can up into the air and nail it about four times out of five with my single BB.

Cars – Cars – Cars

One result of the Great Depression was an abundance of used cars. Automobiles of every variety and model were for sale. The local farmers and anyone who had a steady job could take their pick of fine cars.

While there are gillion cars on the road today, they all look pretty much the same. In the 1930s, however, cars were uniquely designed, and most were built by companies that have long since disappeared. My friends and I liked to sit on the wall of the stone bridge where the Old Philadelphia Pike crossed the creek in Wydnor and see who could name the brand of each car first as it came around the bend. Of course, there were loads of Model A's and even an occasional Model T, but in addition we would typically see brands such as the Franklin (air-cooled), Essex (Super Six), Star, Hupmobile, Stanley Steamer, Studebaker, Marmon, and Willys.

*Left; 1928 Cord Boattail, **right**, 1924 Stanley Steamer, **middle left**, 1929 Hupmobile, **middle right**, 1933 Franklin air-cooled, **bottom left**, 1935 Auburn Speedster, **bottom right** 1935 Stutz Bearcat*

We would even see an occasional Stutz Bearcat with a racing fin at the back, an exotic looking Cord (with rare front-wheel drive), and even a Rickenbacker. That's right. The WWI ace, Eddie Rickenbacker, took a shot at manufacturing cars for a few years after the war, but was apparently unsuccessful.

My parents had a succession of cars of various types, all used, but some quite nice. Our main family car was a 1933 Pontiac straight eight, which ran smoothly and was easy to drive.

At one point my older sister, who was married, had a 1932 Plymouth coupe which was really a menace, as it was equipped with what was called "Free Wheeling." Few people have ever heard of that, as it was a system whereby, when you were going down a hill, the system disconnected the gears from the engine's compression, so that the car just rolled freely. That car did not even have hydraulic brakes, and in the mountainous country where we lived it could get going like a rocket if you didn't ride the brakes down the mountain. "Free wheeling" was so dangerous that it was soon declared unlawful.

Most of the high school kids and some of the farmers had Model A Fords, practical cars that were cheap to run. My parents once bought two of them, a 1929 coupe with a rumble seat ($15) and a 1930 sedan ($25). I think the Model A was the most practical car ever built, especially for teenagers who could easily maintain them. There was nothing you couldn't fix on a Model A.

In one afternoon, the high school kids could drop the oil pan and remove the head, then proceed to replace all of the piston rings and bearings, put in new gaskets, reassemble everything, and have the car running by supper time. Most of the parts would be bought at Pep Boys in Bethlehem. I recall that at one time a set of piston rings for a Model A was on sale for 99 cents, so I would guess that the whole job, including the rings, bushings and gaskets, ran about 10 bucks.

Driving at 13 – Windsor in a Ditch

In that kind of environment it follows that I would learn to drive at an early age, and thus my driving days began when I was 13. It just so happened that my parents had acquired a nice 1930 Windsor. It was a large sedan

1930 Windsor Sedan

in good running condition, with plush seats, and it even had little flower vases of the type found in the back of old sedans in museums.

I had done a little driving with the Model As, which were pretty maneuverable, so one Sunday afternoon my parents decided to try me out with the Windsor, solo. I was doing OK until I turned a corner and found out that the Windsor was not quite so agile, with the result that I drove it in into a deep ditch, where it almost laid on its side. Not a problem; about 10 of the local kids simply climbed on the down side, pushed and lifted while another guy drove it out of the ditch.

Kindly Trooper

I had a Sunday paper route that took me several miles around back country roads. However, as the number of customers grew and the Sunday papers became thicker and thicker, I found it almost impossible to carry the papers on my bike. My parents therefore decided one Sunday that I was proficient enough at driving to let me take the car to deliver the papers.

Normally, that would not have been a problem and I toodled off up the back road, pulled up in front of my first customer, Dr. Eurich, and got out of the car with paper in hand. Lo and behold, there was Doctor Eurich standing on his front lawn talking to a State Trooper in full uniform! My heart jumped into my throat, but I was committed and had no choice but to "guts it out." I walked up to my  customer, said "Good Morning", handed him the paper and turned back to the car. You needed to be 16 to get a license in Pennsylvania and I saw that State Trooper glance at the car and give me a critical once-over. He did not say a word, but all the way to the car I could feel a pair of eyes burning into my back.

Cars in those days all had clutches and some of them weren't so hot, so that you could easily make a jack rabbit start if you didn't coordinate the gas and clutch right. Wow, I thought, this had better be the best start of my life, applied my fullest skills, pulled off a decent start, and drove slowly around the bend. I'm sure that State Trooper knew, but he let it go, as cops were pretty understanding. We weren't thugs, we were simply country kids.

Several times since then, I have told car buffs of my experience driving the Windsor. On every occasion they would say, "You must be talking about a Chrysler Windsor." Not so! Recently I visited the Elliott Car Museum in Jensen Beach, Florida, where a list is on display of almost 2,000 manufacturers (that's right, 2,000!) that built cars in the United States. There it was, the "Windsor" brand, which was in production for only two years, 1929 and 1930. My family must have had one of the last ones built. My nephew Bob Bertolet told me that his family also produced a car at one time. I looked it up at the museum and sure enough, there it was, the Bertolet, another one of the 2,000.

Horse Races and Bookies

Earlier in this narrative, I mentioned my Dad, who was a unique individual with lots of quiet talents. One of them was picking race horse winners. Lots of people in the Steel Company liked to bet on the horses and my Dad was one of them. Like a lot of things, betting was illegal, but it seemed that just about every cigar store in town really had its main business as a Betting Parlor or "Bookie."

Of course, the cops all knew it and played the ponies themselves. Why not? It was their money and if they wanted to bet it that was their business. It was not illegal to spend it or give it away, but I guess society thought otherwise.

Anyway, Dad loved to stop by the local "Bookie" and place a bet or two. It was not a lot of dough, which he didn't have, but a typical bet was two bucks and he would make a bet or so every week. Dad's big thing was studying the racing form and devising schemes to beat the odds, and he loved to tell me about them. There were all kinds of deals about "mudders" (horses that run well with a muddy track) and the other kind, that liked dry tracks, etc.

I particularly remember one scheme which had to do with a combination of handicap weights and pole position of the horse at start. Handicap weights were little bars of lead which were placed in the saddle bags of each horse, as appropriate, to even out the weight of the jockeys that the horses were carrying. I am not sure what Dad's slant was on the handicaps, but the big deal on the pole position was that the horse with the #1 pole position did not win nearly as many times as the odds would dictate, whereas the #2 horse often did really well, all factors considered, as he frequently bounded out ahead of the pole horse and won the race.

I will never forget the day that Dad picked the winner of the 1936 Kentucky Derby. He put $2 on a horse called "Bold Venture" to win, which was indeed a bold venture, as the horse was a 60–1 longshot that had never won a race and was being ridden by a new young jockey. However, as soon as the gates opened, the favorite threw his jockey and in the ensuing mix-up and scramble of racing horses the rest of the likely winners got trapped in the pile up. Good old "Bold Venture" romped home to grab the roses and Dad almost took off to the roses himself, as $120 was a lot of dough in those days!

I never did find out what position his horse started from but I doubt it was the #2 spot, as that was what enabled him to avoid the pack and gallop for the win. However, he must have been under-rated, as he also won the Preakness two weeks later and, after pulling a tendon and being placed out to stud, went on to sire a pair of top-class racehorses: *Assault,* the 1946

Bold Venture

U.S. Triple Crown champion, and *Middleground*, winner of the 1950 Kentucky Derby and Belmont Stakes.

Thinking back on it, maybe I should take up betting the ponies, as Dad sure got a lot of pleasure out of it.

Teenagers and Motorcycles

The Werner family that lived across the road from us in Wydnor had several teenaged sons. They not only acquired a couple of Model A Fords, but also managed to find an old motorcycle. It was a big old Harley flathead, beat-up looking but running well, with plenty of power. My family also had a couple of Model As, so it was commonplace for a group of teenagers and younger guys to gather in the street between the Nebinger and Werner houses and talk shop while tinkering with cars and cycles. I quickly acquired an interest in motorcycles that stayed with me the rest of my life, there rarely being a time when I didn't own one.

There were some downright comical incidents that happened at those gatherings. One time Elwood Werner, or Ellie (of horse sleigh fame), was sitting on his 80-cubic-inch Harley when one of the guys asked if he could take it for a ride. Ellie asked him, "Do you know how to ride?" and the guy said, "Sure."

Ellie cranked up the Harley and turned it over to him. The guy climbed on and twisted the gas grip hard. That bike took off so fast that his entire body left the seat. He ended up hanging onto the handlebars, feeding full gas while the bike accelerated through a nearby field. The poor sap didn't have enough sense to let go, and the bike continued gaining speed while making a complete 180-degree arc.

CRUNCH!   ***Artist John .J. Purdy***

Finally, it roared straight back to where we were standing and slammed broadside into Ellie's Model A, which happened to be up on blocks so he could do some work underneath. It caved in the entire side of the Ford and knocked it completely off the

132

blocks. Fortunately, nobody was underneath the Model A, but the motorcycle was a complete write-off and the rider was lucky to get off with only bruises.

Obviously, the culprit had never been on a motorcycle in his life and I guess that episode dimmed his enthusiasm because we didn't see him around after that. Maybe Ellie gave him some additional encouragement to get lost.

TT Races

My own interest in motorcycles was not dimmed, however, and after my older brother bought a Harley I decided to check out on it, at about age 14. Around the same time I had the opportunity to ride some motorcycles that are quite rare today, including a four-cylinder (in-line) Henderson Super X. I remember particularly that when you sat on the Super X and revved the engine, the change in torque caused the cycle to rock sideways. Of course, I was too young to ride legally. Still, whenever motorcycle races were scheduled in the valley, a couple of my friends and I would manage to find a way to get

there. If we couldn't catch a ride, we rode our bicycles to the event.

One of the favorite nearby racetracks was at Freemansburg, a suburb on the southeast side of Bethlehem. A couple of the local motorcycle clubs had been instrumental in organizing a series of races which they called Tourist Trophy or TT Races. TT races were run on dirt tracks, and no two tracks were the same. Apparently, anybody with any type of bike could enter - and those races were like a Wild West stampede.

Safety was never discussed and some riders wore an old football helmet while some wore none.   For the rest of their outfit, the racers usually wore a pair of leather pants, high top boots, and a shirt with some Harley Davidson or Indian dealer's name and emblem on it.   Almost every motorcycle that raced was either a Harley or an Indian, although once in a while we would see a BMW or an Italian bike, probably a Ducati.   We never heard of a Japanese motorcycle; those were part of the distant future.

The Freemansburg race course had a single straightaway with a 90-degree turn at the end, and followed a winding course thereafter, complete with dips and bumps. Part of the track ran through a clump of woods, where the riders would, for a short time, be completely out of sight of the crowd.   I recall one race where the pack disappeared into the woods and reappeared minus one rider, who must have fallen.   The thundering herd came roaring down the straightaway and disappeared into dust around the first turn, while the fallen rider, who had reappeared, came charging into the turn trying to catch up to the pack. Some clown in the crowd jumped up and pointed, shouting, "They went that way!"

TT Races were downright dangerous and I can recall two occasions when racers were killed when they fell or were hit by other competitors.   The danger also applied to the spectators, as there was virtually no control of where people stood to watch. Believe it or not, spectators would actually cluster on the **outside** of the first turn at the end of the straightaway, which was a ridiculous place to stand. During one race a racer riding an Indian missed the turn and plowed straight into the crowd, which included me. He missed me only by about a foot and banged into a couple of nearby people before coming to a stop, but fortunately no one was badly hurt.

The Widowmaker

The Freemansburg track was at the foot of a steep mountain, and it had the greatest hill climb I have ever seen. The grade of that climb was so steep that you rarely saw a motorcycle make it over the top. My young friends and I were never satisfied to watch from below. We always climbed the hill and sat in the woods near the top to take in the action. Looking down that hill from that vantage point was almost a terrifying experience. Most riders only made it halfway up the hill before flying off. After that point the hill became so steep that riders did not just stall out and fall off, but the motorcycle often went backwards right over the rider's head and tumbled down the hill end-over-end. That hill became known throughout the northeastern U.S. as the "Widowmaker."

I look back upon the races and hill climbs at Freemansburg with very fond memories. It was a wild and wooly business but it exemplified the free spirit of America. Freemansburg was indeed well named. I guess lawyers didn't attend motorcycle races and hill climbs in those days (or if they did, they never dreamed of the bonanza of easy money that awaited them in the future).

Con Men, Scam Artists & Fireworks

About that time my brother, who was three years older than I, became acquainted with a guy named Ollie Hoffman, who lived on the other side of Seidersville hill. Although Ollie was a nice guy, he was one of the biggest con men that I have ever known. Rumor had it that Ollie was a fence for stolen goods and that seems plausible, as he frequently showed up with some odd merchandise and sold it really cheap to the neighborhood teenagers. Once he showed up with a case of 12-gauge shotgun shells and I knew that he did not hunt. My suspicions were boosted when he insisted on driving up a back road into some woods to make the transfer of the case of shells to the guy who bought them.

Ollie had a bundle of creative ideas for making money. For example, one time he picked up some soaps and chemical cleaning agents and went to work mixing concoctions in a barrel in his garage. After a couple of weeks he ordered an assortment of bottles, obtained some printed labels, and - Voila! - announced the sale of "Hoffman's Special Tombstone Cleaner, Guaranteed Not to Stain Marble or Granite Tombstones While Restoring Them to Their Original Luster!"

Ollie didn't always act alone. His entrepreneurial spirit had many facets and, with July looming around the corner, he decided to open a fireworks stand. Because we lived in a pretty wide open area of the country, Ollie decided to locate his stand in Wydnor. Historically, the old blacktop pike near my home had been the only major road to Philadelphia. However, the highway department had recently cut a route through some woods and built a brand new three-lane concrete highway that paralleled the old one. The highway had recently opened but was still largely unfinished, as the guard rails had not yet been installed and there were many places where cars could easily pull off the road. Ollie saw these areas as a natural place to draw from passing traffic and decided to locate his stand right alongside the new highway, with a patch of woods behind to shield it nicely.

For reasons unknown, Ollie decided he did not want to run his own stand. Maybe he was breaking more laws than we realized, or maybe he had some other deals going, but in any case he hired my brother to run the stand, while I also a got a piece of the action as the low-paid helper. Ollie put up a decent frame and canvas stand and loaded it up with zippy fireworks of many varieties.

In those days, there wasn't much interest in those fizzy fountains and pinwheels. Aside from sparklers for the little kids, people wanted fireworks that made a really loud noise. We had plenty of big firecrackers, including some that could take a finger off, as well as skyrockets that went really high and then made a tremendous bang.

Come July 3rd and 4th the stand was doing a pretty brisk business, with many cars pulling off the highway. I could perhaps describe business as "red hot," except that it got a lot hotter after the kid with the lighted sparkler walked up to the stand and some of the sparks fell into the merchandise. Would you believe it, one of those sparks fell right on a fuse which started things off with a bang - and after that all hell broke loose! Trying to put it out was futile, as fireworks were flying everywhere and setting off others.

My brother Bobby and I exited the stand at full speed, heading for the woods, with skyrockets zinging past us and exploding everywhere. In desperation, we ducked behind the largest tree we could find while the rest of the stand went up with a continuing roar, flames shooting 25 feet into the air.

By the time the Se-Wy-Co Model A fire truck arrived, nothing was left but a large black spot on the ground, with smoking debris scattered in every direction. So much for 4th of July celebrations. Ollie wasn't too happy to learn that his investment had gone up in smoke, but no one was hurt. I hardly need to say that we never got paid for the job.

KA-POW!!   *Artist John J. Purdy*

Free Electricity

Moving from con men to scam artists, there was a guy who lived down the street from us who always had some petty racket going and never seemed to pay his bills. One day he was standing talking to a bunch of the guys when he spotted the meter reader from the electric company coming up the road. Without a word he dashed off through a couple of back yards and ran down the steps into his basement. About half an hour later he returned with a smile on his face and rejoined the group. It seems he had rigged a bypass for his electric meter, which was located in the cellar, and barely got there in time to keep the reader from discovering his line.

Stealing electricity can be a little obvious sometimes.
Source: National Safety Council

But wait, it gets better. Even though the guy was getting a fantastic bargain rate on his electricity usage, he didn't pay his bill for several months, and the power company eventually cut him off. How did he solve that problem?

Come midnight, an 18 foot pole with a knife taped on the end came sliding out of his second floor window and extended to the power line which ran in front of his house. A few well-guided jiggles and the insulation was cleared in one small spot. The pole retracted, then reappeared with an alligator clip on the end of a long wire. Presto! Instant power for his house at an even better rate. It just goes to show that for every problem there is a solution if you put your creativity at work!

Chapter Six

WORK PICKS UP – EUROPEAN ORDERS

1938 – 1939

Brother Bob Starts Work at the Steel Company

By 1938, with Europe on the brink of war, production at the Steel Company had increased and the company was hiring. One thing which stimulated business was the fact that Bethlehem Steel was a major producer of artillery and naval shells of many types. That included naval shells for the British Navy and our own navy. (I have recently been told that before the war they were also producing shells for the Japanese Navy, but have no facts to support this. I do know, however, that the steel company was also making castings for aircraft radial engine cylinders for Japan.)

Bethlehem Steel also produced the large gun tubes (barrels) for Navy cruisers and battleships. There was a tall building which contained an annealing tank where the long gun barrels were lowered into an oil bath to cool them slowly and help harden the steel.

My brother, Bob, who had turned 18, applied and got a job at the Steel (as everybody termed it). After the usual stint as a broom pusher/laborer, he became a helper for a guy who was running a metal saw. Bob told me that the saw guy's main function was cutting off bars of steel and other fabrication parts to specified lengths – not exactly a tough job to learn. He also told me about some of the corruption and downright scams that some of the work force were pulling. Here is one of them:

The industrial metal saw was essentially a band saw, with some kind of oil bath to keep it from overheating. One day the guy running the saw was cutting away when he spotted the Rate Setter coming down through the shop.

A Rate Setter was a guy who carried a little book and a stop watch to time and record exactly how much time a typical operation required. The metal saw operation, like a lot of steel company functions, was paid on a per piece basis, so it was in the interest of the company, as well as the saw operator, to make sure that Rate Setter recorded the correct amount of time required to produce each piece. The time that the Setter recorded would then become the basis for the operator's piece-rate of pay.

This particular saw operator, however, had to take it a bit father. As soon as he spotted the Rate Setter coming his way he quickly opened the back of the saw and attached a special spring which took the tension off the blade. When the rate setter actually timed the job, the saw was working away, but apparently taking a long time to cut through the tough steel. However, as soon as the setter moved on, the guy opened the back of the saw, took off the spring, and the saw went through the steel like butter.

Practices like this were commonplace. People skipped out on the job for a couple of hours. Several years later, when I worked in one of the shops, I knew of one guy who actually went to a matinee movie while on a day shift, and got away with it. Also, the people running the time card clocks were constantly fighting a battle to keep people from punching other "phantom" workers in and out.

These were only some of the seeds of destruction which later contributed to the demise of a complete industry.

Over the Mountain to Junior High

After graduating from the eighth grade (with honors, although I have no idea why) at my Seidersville School, I was sent to Broughal Junior High School on the south side of Bethlehem near the Lehigh University Campus. It was a tough school, filled with the sons and daughters of immigrants who came over to work in the steel company, and some of them were not exactly on the refined side.

On my first day in that school I was assigned to a homeroom run by a woman teacher from Texas who was built like a NY Giants linebacker.

When we took our seats that day I naturally took the last seat in a row, and ended up sitting beside a tough looking Hunkie girl (we called all of the immigrant kids Hunkies in those days) A lot of them were Hungarians but we lumped the Slovaks and other nationalities in with them and settled for a single term. Actually, it wasn't meant to be insulting or to put anybody down in any way; it was just a term that everybody used – but it doesn't sound so hot today. Maybe it's a wonder we didn't get beat up a lot!

Anyway, the first words out of that girl's mouth were one of the crudest expressions I ever heard (which I will not repeat) describing rather graphically what that teacher thought of herself. I made the mistake of laughing out loud. The next thing I knew the linebacker came roaring back and slammed my face back and forth about four times between her two hands – sort of like a punching bag except she used open hands instead of fists. My ears were ringing and it brought tears to my eyes.

I guess that teacher wanted to set an early example for the class that she was not going to stand for any guff from smartass kids – and by laughing while she was talking I became Target #1. I never messed around in that homeroom again and you can bet that I didn't go home and whine to my parents about being mistreated. I knew I deserved it.

I found out later that my brother had preceded me in her class by a few years, so I guess maybe he sowed the seeds for the crops (or whops) that I reaped!

Singing Class

One of the required classes in ninth grade was Singing, and the guy that was teaching it was one of the weirdest Lotus eaters I ever met. Why they felt that they have to teach singing in school was beyond my comprehension, and every kid I knew hated that class. It might not have been so bad if we had a teacher who was a regular guy who could laugh it up, but that guy was weird beyond belief. One day he pulled out a sheet of music that I think was from one of the Victor Herbert operettas and insisted that everybody sing the words that went something like:

"Sweetheart, Sweetheart, Sweetheart,

Will you be mine in springtime?"

Sickening! Can you imagine a bunch of teenage kids singing stuff like that? Most of us refused to sing the damned thing but the teacher kept insisting until finally someone tossed a stink bomb against the wall, which emptied the class in a hurry. That was one of the grandest and most satisfying finales I have ever seen!

First Crush

I experienced my first serious romantic crush in ninth grade at Broughal. One day a pretty Irish girl walked into study hall. I was entranced and developed an instant crush that stuck with me for several years. I was a quiet kid, but not a dull clod, and had many female friends, but that was the first time one had swept me off my feet. Ironically, I never made it to first base with that girl.

Later, when we moved on to Liberty High School she had a big thing going with one of the football heroes, but that disintegrated. After the war I actually double-dated with that girl, who was then going steady with one of my best friends, Sheldon Hill, whom everybody called Shelly. He confided in me that he had long term plans for her. I never told him of my interest and wished him success, but that never panned out either.

Oddly enough, that girl never married. Many years later, I heard that she was a Professor at one of the Ivy League Colleges. Maybe she was just a serious scholar. C'est la vie.

Conquering South Mountain

It was about 6 miles over South Mountain to Broughal, and the only practical way to get there was by bike. There was a little country bus that ran to Bethlehem, but it operated only once an hour and you could grow old waiting for it. The mountain was quite steep and was about three-quarters of a mile on the Seidersville side and about a mile and quarter on the Bethlehem side. A couple of us rode it every day, even with snow on the ground, and developed some really tough leg muscles.

Even so, climbing it with a single-speed bike was quite a chore but we developed techniques that made it easier. One trick was to wait for a truck to come laboring up the mountain, then rip out and grab onto the back end for a free ride up the hill. We found a street near the bottom of the mountain where we could wait and get up a good head of steam to enable us to catch the truck and hook on. It worked well except that the truck drivers would see us in the mirror and try to scrape us off by driving close to a pole. We would simply slide all the way behind the truck where it couldn't touch us. Sometimes the drivers would stop and come tearing back, in which case we would simply drop back and turn down the hill. Then when they started back up we would grab on again. Kids can be persistently devilish.

Coming down the mountain side was another matter. We would go as fast as 55 mph, and were clocked at that many times by people in cars. Using some sheet metal, I fashioned a shield that I clamped onto my handlebars to streamline myself. I put a small glass window in the middle and could duck behind it to increase my speed. It also helped to keep behind the shield on the bitter cold days.

We did not have a school bus in Wydnor, but one did operate on the other side of the mountain, heading into Bethlehem. Because the mountain was so steep, the buses and trucks would usually come down in second gear and we would zip by them. One winter day their school bus was heading down the hill with a load of kids going to schools in the south side of Bethlehem. I went shooting by the bus at top speed but didn't reckon on the patch of ice in front of the bus. The bike went out from under me at over 50 mph and I splattered, ending up by sliding for over 100 feet on the side of the bike, with books and paper flying everywhere.

Icy hills presented surprise hazards!

Meanwhile, the bus stopped and the kids on the bus were having a great laugh at my expense. Somewhat chagrined, but uninjured, I collected my stuff, straightened out the handlebars, remounted and cautiously eased my way past the bus again, giving the old finger to the kids as I went by.

Later, when I went to Liberty High School, which was about eight and a half miles away and across the Lehigh River, I continued riding over the mountain every day, summer and winter. To this day, I still have the legs I developed.

Chapter Seven

LABOR PROBLEMS AND THE HIGH SCHOOL YEARS

1939 – 1940

Liberty High School

During the 1930s few families bought homes; they normally rented, as did mine. In 1939, however, my parents finally purchased a house, on North Street, near 10th Avenue in northwest Bethlehem. While I hated to leave the country where I had so many friends, it was a good move all around, as it was much closer to Liberty High School, where I was in tenth grade. Also, it brought me into contact with a whole new circle of teenaged friends, both male and female, and my life took on some completely new slants as we began to range farther afield in the city environment.

Canals, Trains and the Round House

Bethlehem was unique in that it had one of the last commercial canals still operating in the United States. The Lehigh Coal and Navigation Canal had been built in the early eighteen hundreds for general shipping, but was later used primarily to haul coal from the coal regions of Pennsylvania to the hungry mouths of the furnaces at the Bethlehem Steel Company.

Occasionally, a canal boat would come through loaded with coal, and pulled by mules walking along the tow path at the side of the canal. We would sometimes hang out at the canal, watching the boats move through the locks and talking to the lock tender who lived in a little house there. It was a peaceful, pastoral scene, reminiscent of 18th century English canals.

The canal was fairly wide and deep and we sometimes swam in it. While the water may not have been unhealthy from a biological standpoint, it was definitely not the cleanest place to swim. Generations of coal barges had built

Lock Tender's House
Pennsylvania Historical Society

up layers of coal dust into a black muck at the bottom of the canal. It was not particularly bad unless you dived into the stuff; then it could be dangerous. Nevertheless, on hot days it was sometimes convenient to hit the canal. As we got older, we started jumping and diving into the canal from the girders underneath the Hill to Hill Bridge. One day a kid named Ritchie dove off a high beam and did not come right back up. At first we thought he was fooling around, but we then grew worried and a couple of kids went down to check. They found Ritchie with his head stuck in the muck, very much alive but damned worried about running out of air.

Railroads are very interesting places. They exist in areas where few people actually go; hence they are a world of their own. There also is an aura about them, with the smell of creosote, pitch and pine tar.

The Lehigh Valley Railroad, which ran parallel to the Canal,

had a Roundhouse in its Bethlehem yard, and we liked to visit it to watch the operations. It was fascinating to see the huge steam engines roll out onto the turntable, then watch it rotate to deliver the engine off onto another track. Everything was on a massive scale, with wrenches four feet long, and the guys that worked on the engines were nice to us kids. I heard not too long ago that the roundhouse in Bethlehem has actually been preserved, possibly by one of the railroad buff societies. I have not verified this but hope it is true.

As we grew older we got more adventurous and practiced jumping on and off of some moving trains. It was not difficult, but if you were stupid you could get killed.

One thing we found out in a hurry, however, was that the railroad detectives (dicks, we called them). Actually they were Pinkerton men, who patrolled the yards and were not friendly guys. If they caught you the least you could expect was a whack on the rear with a club.

There was a railroad trestle running across the Lehigh River. There were "No Trespassing" signs all over it, but if we wanted a shortcut across the river we simply walked across the trestle. Several times we got caught out on the trestle by moving trains. There was an area in the center of the trestle with some water barrels and places to stand, so you could easily stand there and let the train roar by. However, one time we got caught too far from that section and had to hang onto the beams on the outside of the trestle as the train rolled by. Teenage kids don't worry about stuff like that. Worst case, you have to jump into the river.

Walking the Bridge Railings

The Hill to Hill Bridge was well named. It was fairly long and went from a hill on one side, across the Lehigh River, the Barge Canal, the railroad tracks, and several structures under the bridge, then terminated on another hill. The bridge railings were made of concrete and were about 12 inches wide at the top.

As kids we would sometimes amuse ourselves by walking on the railings. It was easy, and we usually confined our antics to the areas where there was not a high drop-off underneath. However, the people in the cars could not see what was underneath and some of the ladies would go almost hysterical when they saw us. (There were no cell phones that they could use to call the cops in those days.)

One way to add to the drama was to pretend we were losing our balance and actually fall off on the **outside** of the railing, which would send the cars into tire - screeching fits. What they did not know, of course, was that many sections of the bridge had an embankment and a path right on the outside of the wall.

The kid who had apparently fallen off on the outside would pop up with a grin on his face a minute later. Fun!

Artist John J Purdy

Big Trouble in the Rose Garden

There was a pretty rose garden that filled the block between 9th and 10th Avenues along Union Boulevard in Bethlehem. The garden had well-manicured lawns, with benches, where people strolled in the summer, and they provided a nice place for a group of us young teens, both boys and girls, to gather. We played tag football and other games, and also formed a tumbling club, which practiced on the soft lawns. It was at the rose garden that we learned to stand on our hands. Like many such skills, this seemed almost impossible at first, but after some practice we got the hang of it. I soon developed the ability to walk for at least 100 feet or more standing on my hands, a skill that remained with me for many years thereafter. While it didn't have much practical value, it was a good social skill to help wile away the warm summer evenings.

There must be a subconscious urge that impels 15-year-old kids to make trouble for people who are driving by peaceably in their cars. Maybe it is the fact that they are not old enough to drive and can't afford a car in any case. Whatever the reason, that urge got us into a serious jam one evening. A kid named Bill O'Hara, who lived across the street from me on North Street, came up with the bright idea of waiting until a car began to slow for a red light on the next corner, and then throwing a rubber ball at the rear fender. It would make a loud "whoomp" noise. When the poor driver turned around to look, there was Bill, lying by the side of the boulevard in apparent agony. The drivers would stop their cars in a panic and begin running back, at which point Bill would spring up and dash away laughing. It gave the other kids a laugh, but looking back I realize how

155

stupid it was, because teenagers never think that they may give someone a fatal heart attack from the sudden shock.

Our pranks grew even better (or worse) from there. At the Rose Garden, a drinking fountain was located near the side of the boulevard, and sometimes our group would stand around it clowning in typical teen fashion. Once in a while, someone would fill his mouth with water and spray it onto the other kids, leading to the eruption of an all-out water battle. That was OK, as far as it went. But one day as a limousine went by, O'Hara, who had a mouthful of water, decided to squirt it onto the windshield. The problem was, he missed the windshield, the window was open, and the lady inside was dressed in an evening gown. That car came to a screeching halt and a behemoth of a guy came out and charged at us like a hellcat with steam coming out of his ears.

Everyone took off like a shot, but that guy was really fast and singled out O'Hara, me, and a kid named Buddy Swope . We ran as fast as we could down the hill behind the boulevard toward a small valley, but the guy was gaining on us and we knew that anybody he caught would be "dead meat." Here is where my early training (walking in drain pipes) stood us in good stead, because there were some very large drain pipes that carried runoff from the highway down toward a small stream. That was all that saved our bacon, as we ducked into a drain pipe and lost him.

O'Hara didn't pull that stunt again, and the rest of us would not have hung around if he did. Not too long thereafter, however, a few of us were walking down Broad Street and passed the Catholic Church that Bill attended. He said, "Hey, how about waiting for about 20 minutes while I pop in and make my confession." Not long after that Bill emerged from the church with a big smile on his face and said, "Well, I got my slate wiped clean; let's go raise some Hell!" Whatever the formula was, it worked for Bill.

Atlantic City or Bust – on Bikes

Bikes were still very much our main transportation, even though there were lots of trolley cars and buses to ride in the city. I had a friend name Kenny Schlicher, who lived a couple of houses away on North Street. One day, in the summer of 1939, when we were both 15, we were looking for some new excitement and somebody suggested that maybe we should ride to the seashore for some sun and sand. We got out a map and started checking and discovered that it was 120 miles from Bethlehem to Atlantic City, a pretty good stretch for our one speeders. However, considering that we had legs that would take us anywhere, we decided, "Let's do it."

My parents were used to me being a self-sufficient, independent kid, and Kenny's parents also had full trust in him. Actually, I don't think either set of parents bothered to check a map and see how far Atlantic City was, which was OK with us. Anyway, we set a departure date, lubed up our bikes and adjusted the chains, and attached a small bag to our carriers with a sleeping roll, a change of clothes, swimsuits, suntan oil, and a few bucks. We were planning to leave in the morning, but our plans were delayed by a visit by Kenny's relatives. We debated waiting until the next day but our minds were set on departure that day, and we feared something might happen that would cause us to change our plans.

We departed Bethlehem at 6 pm, charged across the Hill to Hill Bridge and up and over South Mountain, and headed down the old blacktop turnpike to Philadelphia, which was 56 miles away.   I don't think it ever occurred to us that we would be riding in the dark at night, but that didn't dim our enthusiasm, so we chugged on. We hit the outskirts of Philadelphia around 11 pm and at midnight rode a ferry across the Delaware River to Camden, New Jersey. Traffic was beginning to quiet down by then, but after some tricky business we managed to find our way out of town to the old Black Horse Pike, which was then the best route south to Atlantic City.

We then proceeded to grind our way down a fairly straight but seemingly endless highway. The most encouraging thing was that somebody had been thoughtful enough to put up signposts, counting off each of the miles to the seashore in descending order. Each mile that clicked off was a small reinforcement. The weather was perfect and we had the highway almost entirely to ourselves. We kept riding until about 2:00 am, when Kenny and I started to get sleepy. We found a nice patch of grass and took about a two-and-a-half-hour nap.

We awoke at 4:30 am with a burning thirst, but nothing was open and we couldn't even find a drink of water. At about 5 am a milkman came along and started dropping off bottles of milk at houses along the road.   Man, that cold milk looked so good, and we engaged in battle with our collective conscience: "Should we or shouldn't we?" "We should" won out when we saw the milkman deliver three bottles of milk to the porch of one home. We reasoned that they wouldn't suffer too much if we "borrowed" one third! That milk was like manna from Heaven!

With our thirst quenched and the sun starting to come up, we took off with a renewed burst of energy and began to clock off the miles. Along the way we began to make friends of a sort. A bus that apparently served a group of the local communities along the highway would pass us about every half-hour. After a while the driver began looking for us, and waved each time he went by. Then, about 25 miles outside Atlantic City, a Chinese man driving a limousine carrying a large family stopped and offered to pick us up and put our bikes on the back of the car. Although everyone in the car was quite nice, we could see the driver's offer would be impractical, and so thanked him and continued on. We rode into the outskirts of Atlantic City just before noon, made our way to the boardwalk, and looked for a place to settle in for the night.

It quickly become clear that Atlantic City was crowded and that the cops would not take kindly to a couple of kids camping under the Boardwalk. We started riding south along the shore and eventually came to a quiet place called Ventnor. There we found a spot where we could camp out under a small boardwalk by the shore. Interestingly, near where we were camping was a huge wooden elephant that was so big it contained a restaurant at the top, accessible by climbing inside its legs. I found out recently that the Ventnor elephant still exists, but has been moved farther away from the beach by the town fathers. Apparently, it fell upon hard times over the years and was close to being torn down, but some townspeople who were admirers of the unique landmark managed to save it.

The Ventnor Elephant.   *Artist: John J. Purdy*

Kenny and I spent two-and-a-half days on that beach, romping in the waves and sleeping under the boardwalk. We got bitten up fairly well by sand fleas, but kids are resilient and we probably played so hard that we could sleep through anything.

One mistake that we made, however, was to ride our bikes in the surf. It was lot of fun, but filled our chains and sprockets with lots of sand, which is a poor substitute for oil.

On the third day we decided to head home in late afternoon. I will never forget that departure. It was raining steadily, we were sunburned, Kenny had a case of sun-poisoning that made him feel sick, and our sprockets and chains were grinding and squeaking as we slogged our way out of town – with 120 miles ahead of us.

We had decided to take a different, more scenic route home, and ride up the west side of the Delaware River towards Trenton. The rain continued, and later that evening we found shelter in a truck garden building piled high with strawberry crates, etc. The mosquitoes had a good feast on us that night, but it was shelter and served its purpose.

By the next day, the rain had ceased but it became hotter and hotter, until the thermometer actually reached 107 degrees and it turned out to be the hottest day on record for a while. Desperate to cool off, we finally stopped and had a nice cooling swim at a place where there was still a section of the old canal that ran alongside of the Delaware. The place was called Washington Crossing, and it was the actual spot where Washington's men had crossed the Delaware in preparation for the attack on the Hessians at Trenton. It was the first time I had ever been there and I found it of particular interest because my direct ancestor, George Nebinger, had been one of those militia men with Washington that fateful night.

Near Frenchtown, we left the river and took a shortcut over the mountain, using a back road to Hellertown. It soon started raining again, and we slogged into Bethlehem in a driving rain at about 9 pm, sunburned, wet, tired, and hungry, but with a lifetime of unforgettable experience in our memory banks.

Joe Ricapito and the High School Orchestra

I had soldiered on with the violin lessons that began when I was nine, so it was only natural that I should try out for the high school orchestra. Frankly, while I liked music, I had lots of other things to do, and was not a real serious student. I have often thought that to play the violin well you really need to have some Hungarian blood, and I didn't have any. My brother had a good friend named Pete Hanson, who would sometimes stop by our back garage when a bunch of the teenagers were hanging out there. Pete was an older man and a solid good guy, who had one squint eye and reminded me very much of Popeye. Pete smoked a pipe and one time he took his pipe out of mouth, and said to me, with a twinkle in his eye, "Eddie, when are you going to give up the fiddle and the bow and take up the shovel and the hoe?" That was probably an astute question.

Anyway, Liberty High School had an outstanding music program under the direction of a fiery Italian named Joseph Ricapito. All the kids referred to him simply as "Joe," but never to his face. Anyone from the area who remembers that time will tell you that Joe Ricapito was a legend in his time, as he not only directed both the high school orchestra and band, but also the renowned Bethlehem City Band, which played concerts at city parks and other civic locations.

Unlike most schools, where the music programs closed down at the end of school season, the Liberty High orchestra and band had weekly practices throughout the summer, so I decided to try out during one of the summer sessions. I was quite capable of making my own application, but for some reason my mother decided that she should take me over to the school and make a personal pitch.

We marched into Ricapito's office, me with violin case in hand, and Mimi started to tell him about my great prowess and how many years I had studied, blah, blah, etc. I was highly embarrassed about the whole deal and couldn't wait to get out of there, but Ricapito, who had heard it all before, went straight for the jugular. He simply took out a sheet of music, set it on the stand, and said one word, "Ply." (Later on I found out that Joe could never say "Play", he always said. "Ply"). Wow, I looked at that music and there were so many 16th and 32nd notes that for a moment I thought that sheet was solid black! It was the "Roman Carnival Overture!" That was one of the worst experiences in my life; I fumbled around for about two minutes until Ricapito simply said, "OK", ushered my hovering mother out, and sat me in the second violin section.

The music played by both the Liberty High orchestra and band was of unusual quality and quite advanced for High School kids. The very first piece of music I practiced with the orchestra was Mozart's G Minor Symphony, a very melodic work. Some of the other selections included Wagner's famous Rienzi Overture, some Respighi, and several Beethoven's symphonies, including the Fifth (or Victory) symphony, and the VI, or Pastorale, as well as dozens of works from light operas. I particularly enjoyed the Pastorale, as there were excellent parts which featured individual instruments such as the oboe and clarinet, and we had some very talented musicians in the orchestra.

Our High School orchestra had about 80 pieces and was actually a full symphony orchestra, which included basses, cellos, violas, a full timpani section, lots of brass, and even a harp and piano. We were particularly fortunate in having a brilliant young first-chair violinist or Concertmeister), whose name, I think, was Stanley Frankenfield. I don't know what his future was, but he was definitely a virtuoso who should have achieved fame in the music world.

Liberty High School Orchestra

Practice sessions with Joe Ricapito were a riot. While he used a regular baton at concerts, for practice sessions he used only a rather thick drumstick. He would stand on his raised wooden stand, hold his hands up in true conductor style and say "Ply ", then proceed to beat cadence on the stand with the drumstick, sometimes using it to point at offending individuals and at other times, when his aggravation reached the boiling point, actually throwing the stick at some trouble makers.

Joe's particular target was very often the timpani section, as drummers are usually natural clowns anyway, and they would go out of their way to get his goat. The brass section, which would occasionally send forth a sour blast, was usually the next serious offender. Sometimes, when things really got out of hand or the music started to fall apart, he would yell very loudly "Ply the Music!" or beat on the corner of the stand furiously with the stick, all the while yelling " No, No, NO, NO" and emphasizing each "NO" with a furious bang on the stand. It got so bad that a corner of the stand started to come apart and this problem had to be solved by covering it with a large brass plate.

Thinking back on my time with the orchestra, there is a beautiful parallel between Joe Ricapito and Geno Auriemma, University of Connecticut's Hall of Fame Basketball Coach, and winner of many National Championships in Women's Basketball – both fiery Italians and both highly successful in their professions. What Auriemma is to women's basketball, Ricapito was to music. Many years later, I was told that after Ricapito's passing someone discovered that he never even had a degree in music! I don't know whether that was true or not, but it didn't matter; he didn't need one!

Christmas at Liberty High

While I am on the subject of music I need to mention the superb Christmas pageants that were put on at Liberty High School. I cannot recall their names, but there were two excellent lady teachers who headed up the choral and other aspects of the music program, and at Christmas time these ladies put on an unforgettable series of pageants.

165

The pageants consisted of a series of scenes from the Nativity, with various events and characters portrayed by selected students in full costume. The scenes were beautifully backlit and the figures posed without moving while the chorus sang music appropriate to each scene. They actually used two choruses. The Senior Chorus was featured in the auditorium, while the Junior Chorus provided a more distant echoing of the music from the halls of the school. The effect was wonderful and moving, and I have never since seen anything to equal it. Of course, such Christmas pageants would probably be banned in schools today, as we live in the age of political correctness. That is, unfortunately, our loss.

Runaway 18-Wheeler

No Driver!
Artist: John J. Purdy

A Coca Cola bottling plant was located on 10th Avenue, about a half a block north of where I lived. Sometimes a large 18-wheeler truck would stop in front of the plant, probably to deliver syrup and other ingredients used in making Coke.

One morning as I was standing on the corner of North Street and 10th Avenue waiting for a ride to school (11th grade), an 18-wheeler slowly rolled through the street intersection, gradually picking up speed and heading downhill toward Union Boulevard. Wow! Suddenly I noticed that there was no driver in the truck! To make matters worse, it was heading straight for a boulevard that was zipping with traffic. Not only that , but 10th Avenue dead-ended on the other side of the boulevard and there were houses there.

My early driver training came in handy and I made a quick decision. I ran and caught up with the truck, jumped on the running board and up into the cab. The engine was not running, but fortunately the brakes and everything worked well, so I simply slowed it down, steered it over and stopped it with the wheels pointing into the curb, set the handbrake and went on my way to school. I thought for a minute about stopping by the Coke plant to tell them where they could find their truck, but decided they would see it, half a block down the street. It never occurred to me that I might have been some kind of hero in the local papers. Looking back, I chuckle to think of the reaction of that careless driver when he walked out of the plant, looked for his truck, and discovered it neatly parked half a block away from where he left it.

Dreams of the Eagle Squadron

While I was in the eleventh Grade at Liberty High, the war in Europe was running at a high pitch and the Battle of Britain was in full swing. I eagerly read every newspaper account of the aerial battles that were taking place, and my particular heroes were the Americans in the Eagle Squadron, who had

Eagle Squadron pilots wore RAF uniforms with this crest.

volunteered to fly Hurricanes and Spitfires with the British Royal Air Force. I know it may sound crazy, but I actually sat in class envying those guys and wondering if the war would end before I could get there.

Life sometimes moves in mysterious ways, because in April 1944, when I was a fully trained P-47 Thunderbolt fighter pilot, I was shipped to England with a batch of other pilots in preparation for the invasion. On the way to my assigned Fighter Group, a truckload full of us stopped by the airbase at Debden, where the Eagle Squadron had been stationed. The base was then occupied by the successor organization, the famous American Fourth Fighter Group, which was flying P-51s. I had been admiring the sleek Mustangs as they taxied by and one of the Squadron Commanders, who might have been a former Eagle, overheard my remarks and actually invited me to join the Group!.   But that's another story.

Caught in a Cavalry Charge

Around the same time I had a rather unique experience which is still stamped into my memory bank.   I related earlier that I was a dedicated model builder, a hobby which remained with me throughout my high school days. While I was at Liberty High School, I had met a guy named Eddie Thoma who was also an airplane nut and a model builder, so we became good friends. It just so happened that we were both building the same free-flight gas model, so he invited me to come over to his house one evening, so that we could work together. For those readers who happen to be old time model builders, we were working on a design called a Goldberg "Zipper", a model with a pylon-mounted wing of 6 foot span, powered by a .60 cubic inch engine.

Eddie lived on the south side of the Lehigh River, near the Bethlehem Steel plant. I went there at about 7PM that evening, and Eddie introduced me to his parents, who were of Greek descent. They were lovely people, who welcomed me warmly to their home, and started our model building activities off with a nice chunk of cake.

It was 1940 and the Bethlehem Steel Company was in the midst of the last of the great labor strikes, which had plagued the firm over the previous four or five years. We knew that  there was lots of striker activity going on, but the people around there had become rather accustomed to labor agitation, and did not pay too much attention to it. This particularly strike, however, had gotten out of hand and gone well beyond the usual picket activity, with the shouting and name calling etc. Roaming gangs of strikers had targeted all of the parking lots on the side of the hill facing the steel plant and, assuming that any cars parked there belonged to non-union "scabs" working in the plant, rolled over hundreds and set fire to many of them.

Now, to fully grasp the scenario I am about to relate, a basic understanding of the geography of the neighborhood is helpful.

Basically, the steel company ran for miles alongside the Lehigh River in South Bethlehem.   Third Street paralleled the plant running just south of the plant at the base of South Mountain. A long block up the hill, Fourth Street paralleled Third Street, and running in between the two streets was a double set of railroad tracks. Eddie's house was on a cross street running up the hill from Third Street to Fourth Street and just above the railroad tracks. I am not sure but believe it was called Buchanan Street.

Eddie and I were working away and could hear a certain amount of commotion.   Looking out the window, we noticed that several hundred strikers had gathered in front of a saloon up on Fourth Street. Apparently, some of them were getting pretty well liquored up, because they had started breaking street lights and we noticed a couple of cars burning in the distance.   What we didn't know, however, was that the Governor of Pennsylvania had called out his special horse-mounted troop of riot police as strike breakers, and that about fifty or more of those guys were massing on the railroad tracks about a hundred yards down the street from Eddie's house.

Along about 9:30 PM, Eddie and I decided to pack it in, and take a look at what was going on outside.   We popped out of his front door and for the first time saw the troop of strike breakers, right down the street.   I said, "Let's go look", and we started walking down the middle of the street toward the troopers. They were all great big guys, apparently specially selected for tough jobs. Earlier in history, those special troopers had played an important role in squashing some really vicious labor riots in the coal regions of Pennsylvania, where the most militant strikers were known as the "Molly McGuire's," as featured in the movie of the same name.   Each was in full uniform including a special helmet, reminiscent of the Balaclavas worn by the British in the Crimea, during the Charge of the Light brigade, and each was carrying a long club – apparently designed to massage some heads from horseback.

Speaking of the Light Brigade, we got halfway down to the horsemen when the head guy suddenly yelled "Charge!"   I couldn't believe it, because there we were, halfway between the cavalry on one side and their targets, the strikers, up the street! We ran as fast as we could to scuttle out of the way, but that street was not really wide enough for that many guys on horses at a gallop.

Artist: John J Purdy

171

We barely managed to squeeze over to one side, but not before one trooper galloped by, narrowly missing us and yelling, "Get the Hell out of here, kid," then reached down and gave me a good whack on the rear with his club. The thundering herd then roared by and proceeded to rush the guys up the street, who scampered for their lives in every direction.

That's how I learned, first hand, what it feels like to be caught in the middle of a cavalry charge!

There is an ironic aftermath to that episode. I never saw Eddie Thoma after high school graduation, but a few years later I heard his story. Like most of us airplane nuts he had pursued a flying job in the war and earned a pair of silver wings as a multi-engine pilot.

In 1944 he was copilot on an 8th Air Force B-17, flying out of England to bomb targets on the Continent. I never knew this at the time, and may well have actually escorted his Group on some missions, as one of our jobs was to perform high altitude escort for the bombers in the 8th Air Force, flying P-51 Mustang fighters.

In 1944 Eddie's Group was on a bombing mission to a target in Germany, when his B-17 took a major hit from German Flak. The Flying Fortress made it back to England, but Eddie, who had been seriously wounded, died from his injuries on the way home. I am left with a fond memory of a good guy and a great friend.

Chapter Eight

TEEN-AGE FUN AT THE BACKYARD GARAGE AND ELSEWHERE

1940 - 1941

While living on North Street we had a nice backyard garage, with the entrance on the alley behind our house. My brother, who was into working on cars and motorcycles from an early age, had a very nice workshop there. Teenagers are naturally interested in cars, trucks, motorcycles and mechanical things, so the garage became a hangout for a diverse group of young people. There was lots of innovative rebuilding of cars and cycles, accompanied naturally by a liberal portion of colorful language in some imaginative varieties. We also had a barrel of fun playing tricks on each other, so that there was not a day went by without another good caper. Here are some examples:

173

The Spark-Coil Trick

There was a natural pecking order among teenage kids. Some were accepted by all as natural leaders and were considered as smart guys. Others were sort of average parts of the gang. Then there was a third stratum of kids that were a bit kooky. I don't mean crazy, they were OK kids and we actually liked them, but they weren't the sharpest knives in the rack. To put it another way, they were somewhat gullible, and hence became perfect targets for practical jokes and tricks.

There was one such kid who liked to jump into the front seat of my brother's 1936 Oldsmobile, or in any other interesting vehicle he saw, and paw everything in sight. I guess he just liked cars. Anyway, he was a natural target, and the guys set him up for it.

My brother, Bob, had a Model T spark coil that he found in a junkyard. Hooked to a 6 volt car battery, that thing could give you a kick like a mule. One day Bob rigged some fine wires in the front seat of the Olds, and hooked up the spark coil to the battery with a simple "On–Off" switch.

Sure enough, here came the sucker, who popped into the front seat of the Olds, right on cue. Bob waited till he got himself settled in very comfortably and hit the switch. There was a "Yow" and that kid came out of there like a rocket!

Everybody had a good laugh at that, including the victim. However, he always asked permission thereafter.

John Palmer and the Tooth Devil

Among the high school kids that used to hang out at our backyard garage was a young guy named John Palmer. John was a really fun-loving guy, with a bizarre sense of humor, and he would do funny imitations of everything and anything on the spot, making people laugh.

One time John had a nagging toothache which had been dogging him for about a month, until he finally got it pulled by the dentist. Right after that John showed up at our garage with the offending tooth in hand.

We had one of those huge iron vices on the workbench in our garage and John headed straight for it. He put the tooth in the giant vice and slowly and deliberately tightened the vice on it until the tooth was crushed, all the while saying, "Now you tooth devil, I am going to get even with you and give you some of your own medicine!"

Then he turned to me and said gleefully, "Eddie, can't you just see that nerve writhing in agony and screaming in pain?" What a clown!

Oddly enough, John Palmer really wanted to be an undertaker. I really think what he wanted the most was to possess one of those long black limousines, as he loved those things.

I don't know whether John ever achieved his ambition, as the war sent us all on different paths, but he probably did. He had the name for it.

175

The 'Rider'

When we were seniors in High School, there was a 16 year old kid named Eddie Sachs who started hanging out at the garage. Eddie actually lived in Center Valley, outside of Bethlehem, but somehow we got acquainted. The common denominator was that several of us had old Harley Davidson motorcycles that we had scrounged someplace, and Eddie was fanatic about putting new pieces of chrome on his bike, any chance he got. Most motorcycle riders then wore those very wide belts, which were called Kidney Belts, as they were supposed to provide protection from pounding up and down, and one day Eddie showed up with a dandy new one.

Eddie considered himself a pretty hot rider, so one time when he left the belt at the garage we got some of those silver studs and put them on, spelling out "Rider" in big letters. Eddie was delighted with that epithet and thereafter we always referred to him with tongue in cheek as "The Rider." Eddie and I used to ride together quite a bit and we had developed a pretty good level of proficiency at standing up on the seat, no hands, while cruising along. Unlike modern motorcycles, which have spring loaded gas throttles, early Harleys did not have a spring loaded throttle and the gas would remain where you set it after you took your hands off.

Standing on the seats while going straight ahead was pretty easy, but one day when we were cruising down Union Boulevard, Eddie decided to stand up, and then turn around in flight. We weren't going very fast, but that was still not a good idea, because Eddie ended up bouncing down the highway, sans helmet, while his bike continued another hundred feet before bashing itself and ruining a lot of his fancy chrome. Fortunately, he wasn't hurt, but that cooled down our acrobatic adventures.

There is an interested sequel to the "Rider" anecdote. After the war, Eddie and I spent a lot of time riding around together. Sometimes he would borrow his parents' car, which was a nice souped-up Ford V-8. Eddie had a definite heavy foot on the gas, and that car took a lot of punishment. Most times, however, we would ride our motorcycles out to parks and fairs, usually with girl passengers on the buddy seat, etc. and it was a lot of fun.

At the Allentown Fair they always had the guy that rode his motorcycle around in a huge wooden barrel, making lots of noise and snatching dollar bills that the customers held out as he roared by. Eddie really enjoyed that. Later, when I was recalled and went back into the military service I heard that Eddie actually got a job riding the cycle in the barrel, then graduated to midget race cars at Dorney Park. Sometime thereafter he also married a girl named Nancy McGarrity, who lived a block away and was an occasional hanger out at our garage.

I don't know the exact sequence thereafter, because I was gone for many years, but I know that Eddie gradually worked his way up in the racing world and by the fifties was one of the favorites at Indianapolis. Eddie never won Indy, but he came very close and finished second to A. J. Foyt in 1961. He had a brilliant record in racing and was a great crowd pleaser.

Here is a synopsis of his racing record:

Eddie Sachs

Race car driver Eddie Sachs was known as the Clown Prince of Auto Racing, but was far from a clown when it came to winning races. Eight USAC National Championship wins, 10 USAC Sprint Car wins. USAC Midwestern Sprint Car Champion, 1958. 8-time starter of the Indianapolis 500. Indianapolis 500 Pole Winner, 1960, 1961. Best Indianapolis 500 finish, 2nd, 1961. Killed in a fiery crash on the 2nd lap of the 1964 Indianapolis 500, which also claimed the life of Dave MacDonald and injured Ronnie Duman and future 3-time 500 winners Johnny Rutherford and Bobby Unser. (Bio by Jim Adams)

Source: Wikipedia

In 1964, while I was stationed in Maryland, I was watching the Indy 500 on television, when very early in the race, a rookie named MacDonald hit the wall, bounced back onto the track, and Eddie hit him broadside. Everybody had a full fuel load and there was a tremendous ball of fire. Both Eddie Sachs and Dave MacDonald were killed, and three others drivers were injured in the five car crash, including two future Indy winners.

Wacky Model Flying Experiences: Model Eating Tree

Several times in this narrative I made reference to various model airplane building activities. During my high school years, this hobby continued to occupy my spare time, and at some point along the line a group of us formed a club called the Bethlehem Aero Aces. That club grew rapidly until we had about 50 members, with ages ranging from 10 to 60. It was a great recreational activity and members built model airplanes of many sizes and varieties.

There were lots of big open fields in the Lehigh Valley then, where we could fly models, and the farmers did not chase us unless they had crops actively growing. Consequently, on nice Sundays a group of us would meet in some field and stage a little impromptu contest. Radio control was in its early days, so the major activity was gas powered free flight models, which were specially designed to climb like a rocket, then, glide very efficiently. We had a timer on the engine which would cut it off after only 10 – 15 seconds, but during that very short period, a good free flight model could be at least 200 feet in the air.

Because they were such highly efficient gliders, it was entirely possible that a model could catch a hot air updraft (or thermal) which would take it higher and higher, until it became a dot in the sky.

For this reason, I always glued a little plague on the side of my models, with my name, address and phone number. While I lost a couple completely to thermals, I actually had one returned to me by a nice man who found it in his cornfield 20 miles away, and drove to my house with it.

The people in the club were a great bunch of diversified people who had one thing in common. We were all airplane nuts of some type of other, and there surely were some characters in the club.

One Sunday a guy name Paul Kuhnsman, whom we called PK, had his model land in the very top of a high, unclimbable tree. The wind was blowing and the branch was moving, but that model was stuck fast.

Paul's solution? After studying the situation he jumped in his father's car, which he had borrowed, drove home, and also borrowed his father's 30 – 30 rifle with a telescopic sight. Six well placed shots took the branch off neatly, and on its way down the model came loose and made a fairly soft landing, with minimum damage.

A few years later PK joined the Air Force. Somebody must have discovered his talent as a deadeye shooter because he became an Aerial Gunner on B-17s in the 8th Air Force, and was credited with bagging two Fw-190 fighters.

Chasing a Model with a Cessna

Then there was the time that a guy named Eddie Tefs** launched a red-hot design of his own that took off like a homesick angel, promptly hooked a thermal and started climbing. We were used to chasing them on foot and got a lot of exercise that way. But this one was really taking off. I was riding my brother's motorcycle that day, so Eddie jumped on the back and we started chasing it, as it got higher and higher while drifting downwind. We chased it for several miles until it started to go across the Lehigh River, but there was no bridge in sight. By luck we were close to a little airport so we dashed into the airport to see if we could find somebody willing to chase it with an airplane. (We had invested a fair amount of money and time in those models, and an efficient contest model was something we didn't want to lose.)

I had not begun my own flying lessons yet and did not know anybody at the airport; however, as luck would have it there was a pilot hanging loose with a four seater Cessna, and he said, "OK, let's go." Eddie and I jumped into the back seat and the guy cranked up the bird and took off. Believe it or not, after some searching we actually caught up to that model at 1,100 feet! The pilot then proceeded to do a series of stalls over the model, so that the prop wash caused it to spin out and drift down before recovering. We tracked that model across the Lehigh River and watched it descend to some bushes right near a high tension tower on the very top of a mountain, and marked the spot carefully. The pilot was kind and charged us the minimum for a half hour of flying. I think it was a unique experience for him and he enjoyed it.

181

We then jumped on the motorcycle, went across the nearest bridge we could find, rode up the side of that mountain until the road ended, parked the bike, proceeded to plod our way up to the top of that mountain, and after a relatively short time searching found the model completely unscathed. The whole episode occupied almost a full afternoon, but Eddie Tefs went home happy with his hot performance model. I got some further appreciation of flying and knew that I had to learn to fly.

** Eddie Tefs became a B-24 pilot and served as an Instructor in the Training Command during the war.

Chapter Nine

AFTER GRADUATION

1941 -1942

In June 1941 I graduated from high school at the age of 17. My first job was as a shelf stocker at one of the local "five and ten" stores in South Bethlehem. It lasted exactly one week. The boss came to me and asked me to verify my birthday and I did. He said, "I am sorry, you are doing a good job but we are going to have to let you go." Because of the recently passed Fair Labor Standards Act, all of their employees had to be at least 18. Somebody had failed to check my birthday on my application. It was the same way with all of the bigger companies; you could not get a decent job unless you were 18.

The Sweat Shop

That left me looking for something to do, and my friend, Frank Rice, was in the same boat. The two of us ended up working for a woodworking company called Kurtz Brothers, located just off of Union Boulevard in Bethlehem. I had heard of sweat shops, but that was my first experience working in one.

Frank and I started out unloading lumber from a freight car. You would not believe how much lumber is contained in one freight car or how heavy that stuff can be. What made it really tricky and dangerous was that the company had a small spur track which ran over a little bridge across a ravine and into the factory. We had to transfer the lumber from the freight car onto a rail hand car and push it into the plant. That wouldn't have been so bad, but the little spur line over the bridge was broken in about three places and we had to rig all kinds of crazy supports to keep it from collapsing. Each time we went across we held our breath, hoping it wouldn't collapse and bury us under three tons of lumber.

We survived that ordeal and my next job was as helper for a guy who ran a large band saw. That guy's job was to cut floor boards for trucks from a 4 X 8 sheet of ¾ inch plywood, and mine was to stand at the end supporting the boards at the proper height so that he could manipulate them in the band saw. Anyone who has lifted a sheet of ¾ inch plywood knows that those things are pretty heavy. Single sheets weren't so bad, but sometimes we had to clamp as many as four boards together so he could cut them at one time. I was a pretty strong and wiry seventeen year old, but that was really punishing, as my wrists and arms would be burning like fire by the time I was able to let go of the boards. You'd think that anyone with a little ingenuity would have gotten a small adjustable dolly on casters to do the job, but that was not to be.

Now, here is where it really gets good. The factory was owned by two old Kurtz brothers who stood around all day watching the workers like hawks to make sure that nobody wasted any valuable time. Considering that we were making the astounding sum of 40 Cents an hour, ($16 bucks a week), that would not have been too much of a risk. However, whenever we stopped for even a minute, one of the brothers would quickly hand us a broom so we could stay busy sweeping up.

I can't recall the name of the guy running the saw, but he was a really good egg and a real avid jazz fan. He would sometimes dance around the saw singing some crazy song and would say to me something like, "Nebbie, let's go out to the Rainbow Room and see Charley Spivak on Saturday night." The Rainbow Room was a big dance place located right across the street from Central Park. We were at the height of the big band era, and Spivak was one of many big bands that came there, including Harry James, Glen Miller, and the Goodman brothers.

I did not mention that the two Kurtz Brothers had a nephew who was a serious understudy of their labor management techniques. One day, one of the workers was running a radial arm saw, cutting pieces of wood to specified lengths. The nephew, who was watching carefully, remarked, "No, no, that is not the way to do that, you're much too slow. Let me show you." He demonstrated his technique alright, and in the process took two fingers off of his left hand.   It was a pretty bad scene, and it may sound mean spirited, but it is not too much of a stretch to understand why some people in that factory had a hard time keeping a smile off of their face.

After a while I landed a much plusher job at Kurtz Brothers – building wooden desks.   Pearl Harbor had not taken place yet, but Europe was deeply at war and the U.S. War Department was beginning to expand. (They did not call it the Dept. of Defense then; it was the War Dept.) One thing they needed quickly was lots of desks for the paper shufflers, and Kurtz Brothers was eagerly filling that vacuum.   Now, if I asked you to guess how long it took for me to build a high-quality Kurtz Brothers desk, what would you guess? An hour? Half an hour? Actually, the correct answer is 8 minutes!

That's right; there was a big jig on the bench, and there were bins filled with all of the parts, cut to shape.   My working tools were simply a pot of glue and a mallet.   After learning the correct sequence, I would grab a piece, dip it in the glue, stick it into the jig, give it a tap and move on. I think I may have been the world's fastest desk builder! The assembled desk would then go to another set of guys who swabbed some finish on it and put it in a room to dry.

Rich Airport and the 'Dragon Lady'

About that time I decided to put some of my hard-earned money to work, learning to fly. There was a small grass airfield along the highway to Easton, about 8 miles east of Bethlehem. It was run by a guy named Cyrus Rich, whom everybody called Cy. Rich Airport was typical of small country airports; on most any given day you could find a guy working on an old biplane or whatever, often with a bucket of oil under the engine and parts spread across a workbench. On weekends, the usual crowd of airplane buffs, pilots and hangar flyers was always to be found, telling jokes and tall tales about flying.

Taking the bit in hand, I went down to the airport and spoke to Cy, who referred me to a Flight Instructor named Percy Jermyn (I am not sure of the spelling and can't find my original Log Book). Percy had a fifty horsepower Piper Cub, (with single ignition) and agreed to take me on as a new student for the amazing sum of 8 bucks an hour, including gas for the Cub, which was pretty cheap in those days.

He turned out to be a really excellent instructor, who demonstrated some of the nuances of flying that the average pilot does not visit.

We started out with the usual routine of straight and level flight and turns, followed by the complete range of stalls, power on and power off, both straight ahead and in turns, as well as accelerated stalls in a turn. Then Percy taught me how to coordinate pitch and power to coax the most out of the Cub's puny engine with finesse. That included Chandelles, which comprised a gradual climbing turn so that you reached maximum altitude and minimum control airspeed at the same time that you completed a 180 degree turn, a coordination challenge to execute perfectly.

This was followed by Lazy Eights, which were kind of like extensions of a Chandelle, except that you performed a series of continuous climbing and descending turns right and left, forming continuing eights in the sky.

The Cub had a basic needle and ball "Turn and Bank Indicator", which showed whether you were using the correct angle of bank to avoid side-slipping in turns. Doing Lazy Eights is a great exercise in smoothness and finesse, as you are continually changing control movements to keep the ball centered, indicating that you are perfectly coordinated at all times.

One exercise that Percy liked to demonstrate was called Pylon Eights. He would look for a nice straight road with the prevailing wind blowing directly across the road at a 90 degree angle. He would then select two barns or other structures to serve as pylons on the road, each equidistant from a center point on the road.

You would start out going straight across the road at the center point, and then make a gradual 360 degree turn back across the road and continuing around until you crossed the road straight and level at your original starting point, then reversing the turn and going in the other direction.

That sounds relatively simple. However, as the wind was blowing straight across the road, in order to keep your circles on each side equidistant from the road and pylons you had to shallow your bank on the upwind side and steepen it on the downwind side.

Acrobatically speaking, there wasn't much you could do with a Cub, although Percy taught me the fine points of tailspins and coaxing the Cub over the top in a fairly decent loop. He was probably bored with that stuff, so that at the end of an hour, after we landed, he liked to give the hanger flyers a little show, by giving the engine a burst of power, slamming the stick over to the side and "yoiking" the Cub up on one wheel, then taxiing in (pretty fast) with one wheel in the air.

One of the beauties of a country airport was that there were not a lot of CAA Inspectors waiting to catch you doing stuff like that. It was Civil Aeronautics Authority in those days. At that time the Civil Aeronautics Authority was responsible for air traffic control, safety programs, and airway development

Artist: John J Purdy

It just so happened that shortly before I started my lessons the "powers that be" had decided to ban all civilian flying of light aircraft within a certain distance from the East Coast. I think it was 65 miles, and believe it had something to do with air defense of the coast.

The net result of this was that it brought some of the New York City and Jersey people over to fly out of Rich Airport, which was just over the limiting line.

Some older readers may remember Milton Caniff's comic strip of the 1930s, *Terry and the Pirates*. (It first appeared in the Sunday funnies, and later comic books, and even became a TV series.)

The Dragon Lady

One of the cast of unique characters that appeared in the strip was a cute and curvy woman with some distinctly oriental features called the *Dragon Lady* – also known as Madam Deal or Lai Choi San. She was the leader of a pack of Chinese pirates that were continually giving the U.S. heroes a hard time.

Anyway, Caniff's real model for the strip, who lived in NYC, had brought her airplane over to Rich field and became one of the weekend regulars. She really did look amazingly like the comic strip *Dragon Lady*.

Hanger scuttlebutt had it that she wasn't such a hot pilot, but that didn't matter, as she had the spirit and was one of the gang.

From Wikipedia, the free encyclopedia

The Dragon Lady, also known as Madam Deal, was a well-known character in the popular U.S. comic strip Terry and the Pirates, created by Milton Caniff, and in the movie serial, comic books, and TV series based on the comic strip. Her "real" name was Lai Choi San.

The Dragon Lady first appeared in the Sunday strip story in 1934. She began as a stereotypically beautiful, seductive, and evil Asian, but as the comic strip became more realistic, the character of the Dragon Lady grew more complex. Fans of the strip recall her passionate love for Pat Ryan, and the time she taught Terry how to dance.

In the years leading up to World War II, she became a heroic though Machiavellian figure leading the resistance against the Japanese invasion of China.

According to Milton Caniff she was modeled from a real person, as were all of Caniff's characters, in this case a succession of them, starting with professional model Phyllis Johnson.

I soldiered on with my weekly lessons and, after seven hours, Percy soloed me. I was 17 years old, and that was one of the most memorable days of my life. Anyone who flies will tell you that it is a strange experience to be up in an airplane with only yourself at the controls for the first time. You only experience it once.

There was an interesting sequel to my Rich Airport experience. One of the chief jokesters at Rich Airport was CY's younger brother, Stuart, or Stu. In early 1943 I reported to the Classification Center at Nashville, Tennessee as an Aviation Cadet. At that stage I was a long way from actually becoming a military pilot, because that was the place where they sorted out all of the applicants with a series of tests and psychological interviews to determine who would be selected as a potential pilot, navigator, bombardier, or be "washed out" of the Cadets altogether. Those who were washed out were usually reassigned to training as a ground mechanic, or possibly as an enlisted member of a flight crew, such as an aerial gunner.

The first day at Nashville, all of us aspiring pilots were assigned to a squadron barracks, each with about 20 new guys. I walked in, plunked down my bag, and there, two beds away, was Stu Rich! There were lots of fun tricks that took place in that barracks, and true to form, Stu Rich soon became the chief clown and jokester. There was the usual pack of ordinary tricks, such as "short sheeting" or otherwise sabotaging other guys' beautifully made up beds, so they would get "gigged" by the inspecting officer. However, Stu had to take it a peg farther.

Most of the cadets in that barracks were from the Northeast but there were a couple of "good old boys" from the Deep South. As soon as people became a bit better acquainted, Stu targeted those southern boys, organized a marching troop of Yankees, and marched everybody up and down the barracks, playing Kazoos and singing "As we go marching through Georgia" ** Believe me; those southern boys did not take kindly to that, one bit. It was not too many years after the Civil War then, and old wounds heal slowly. Of course, it was all meant in the spirit of fun, and we were all on the same side, but there were times when it appeared that we might re-ignite the War Between the States!

I never saw Stu after leaving the Classification Center and have no idea what happened to him in the war.

** Lyrics from the song "Marching Through Georgia," written by Henry Clay Work at the end of the American Civil War in 1865.

Pearl Harbor Day, December 7, 1941

The Sunday of December 7, 1941 was an unusually warm day for the middle of winter. I was sitting on the front steps of our house, soaking up the sunshine, when a friend named Charlie Cope – a top football player at Liberty High – walked up and said to me, "Ed, you might get your chance to fly fighter planes yet; the Japs just bombed Pearl Harbor! My next question was, "Where is Pearl Harbor?"

Our whole country changed after that.

Off to Join the RCAF

Exactly 29 days later, on January 5, 1942, I turned 18. My generation had arrived just in time to become cannon fodder, but we did not view it that way.

My real ambition had been to become an Army Air Corps pilot, but at least two years of college were required to join the Corps – a matter of much frustration to me. Nevertheless, I considered myself lucky to have obtained my flying license before then, because civilian flying was soon virtually curtailed except for paramilitary-type programs such as ROTC training.

I did not want to be a "ground pounder," as the non-flying Army guys were called, and considered trying to grab a quick year of college, but events were moving too swiftly for that. Then one day I heard there were opportunities in Canada, provided you had some flying experience, of which I had a little. I discussed this option with my friend Frank Rice, and we decided to head to Canada to join the Royal Canadian Air Force.

We gathered up a few bucks, packed a bag between us, and started hitchhiking to Canada. While we had always had good luck hitchhiking in the past, on this particular day, May 15, 1942, there was scarcely a car on the road. It turned out to be the first day of gasoline rationing on the East Coast, and no one was traveling more than a couple of miles.

The Office of Price Administration had issued stickers to be affixed to a car's windshield, and gas could only be bought in limited quantities, based upon need. The "A" sticker was issued for non-essential use, and the owner could purchase only 3-4 gallons per week. The "B" sticker, which indicated that the car was being driven for use essential to the war effort, allowed the owner to purchase 8 gallons per week. This sticker was allowed to be used by industrial war workers.

Clearly, nobody was heading to Canada; in fact, nobody was going anywhere very far that day. Frank and I stood on the highway outside Allentown for over three hours without being able to thumb a single ride. We finally gave it up and made our way home again. Fate is sometimes decided by unusual twists.

Gas Rationing during WWII

In May 1942, the U.S. Office of Price Administration (OPA) froze prices on practically all everyday goods, starting with sugar and coffee. War ration books were issued to each American family, dictating how much any one person could buy. The first nonfood item rationed was rubber. The Japanese had seized plantations in the Dutch East Indies that produced 90 percent of America's raw rubber. President Franklin D. Roosevelt called on citizens to contribute scrap rubber, old tires, old rubber raincoats, garden hoses, rubber shoes, and

bathing caps. The OPA established the Idle Tire Purchase Plan, and could deny mileage rations to anyone owning passenger tires not in use. The national maximum "Victory Speed" was

195

35 miles an hour. "Driving clubs," or carpools, were encouraged. A magazine ad declared, "Your Car is a War Car Now."

Gasoline was rationed on May 15, 1942 on the East Coast and then in December, nationwide. The OPA issued various stickers to be affixed to the car's windshield, depending on need. To get your classification and ration stamps, you had to certify to a local board that you needed gas and owned no more than five tires.

The "A" sticker was issued to owners whose use of their cars was non-essential. After you handed the pump jockey your mileage ration book coupons and cash, the attendant could sell you 3 or 4 gallons a week, no more. For nearly a year, A-stickered cars were not to be driven for pleasure at all.

The green "B" sticker was for driving deemed essential to the war effort; industrial war workers, for example, could purchase eight gallons a week.

Red "C" stickers indicated physicians, ministers, mail carriers and railroad workers, and incidentally were the most counterfeited type.

'T" was for truckers, and the rare "X" sticker went to members of Congress and other VIPs.

Enlisting in the Army Air Corps August 1942

As discussed above, when America first entered the war you still needed two years of college to get into the Army Air Corps' Aviation Cadets, or the Navy's Flying Training program. However, with the rapidly expanding forces structure of the U.S. Armed services, the decision was soon made to drop the strict college requirement, but all applicants had to pass a pretty stiff educational test, in order to be accepted in the programs.

This was good news to me, and in August of 1942 I went to Allentown and applied. There were about a hundred applicants and most of them were a couple of years older than I was. Also, I found out that a lot of them had some college under their belt, so I was worried that maybe I wouldn't cut it, as the test was graded competitively.

We sat down to about a two-hour test, which included some stuff that I was a bit shaky on, but most of it was geared toward your mechanical IQ, as well as finding rational solutions. I had a pretty logical mind, but some of the questions were designed to be a bit tricky, so I left there wondering how badly I might have done. The next day the guy who administered the test called me up and told me that I had scored second highest in the whole pack! I couldn't have been happier.

There followed a really comprehensive physical exam in which they checked everything, but paid special attention to vision and depth perception. I had one very amusing experience when a guy was flashing a whole series of cards to test whether I might be color blind. I was zipping through them pretty well, when there was one which I looked at and did a double take, because it was pretty faint on the card. I said to the guy, "Could I take another look at that one? It's a 67, I'm sure, but it is real tricky." The guy answered, "I wouldn't know, I can't see any of em, I am totally color blind!" Talk about a square peg in a round hole - that was typical of early Army personnel assignments.

On August 10, 1942, the group of us who had met all requirements were called to Allentown and stood on the steps of the Court House being sworn into the U.S. Army Air Corps as Aviation Cadets. Our expectation was that we would quickly be leaving for our first training base, but we were in for a real surprise. The Officer announced to us that we were now officially in the Army's Reserve, but that due to a large backlog in the training commands, we would have to wait at least 7 months before actually being called to active duty!

Meanwhile, my friend Frank Rice had joined the U.S., Marine Corps and was destined to fight in many of the Pacific Island landings with the First Marine Division.

Chapter Ten

WORKING IN THE BETHLEHEM STEEL COMPANY

(Delayed Call to Active Duty)

1942 - 1943

Shop Clerk and General Factotum

After that I decided that, while I waited, I might as well get a job as a defense worker, The Steel Company was hiring, so I applied for a job and got hired as a Shop Clerk in the Shell Shop. That was a shop about a city block long where they made all kinds of shells and bombs.

My job was to run errands for the boss of the Shell Shop, who had a second floor office right in the plant, with windows where he could look out over all of the machines on the floor. Of course, he had a number of subordinates who headed up individual aspects of the manufacturing process, and he coordinated the whole deal.

Communications were not easy, as they are today, and he would send me out into the plant to take messages to various departments or individuals. It was really interesting, because I got to observe first-hand every single type of operation necessary to complete the production process.

16 inch shell handling room on USS Massachusetts.
Source: U.S. Navy

There was a variety of huge drop forges which banged out the basic shapes of certain types of bombs, and there were hundreds of metal lathes on which the steel shells of every size were machined, starting with 5-inchers, and running up through the complete range of artillery shells, including 15 and 16-inch naval shells.

Most of the 15-inch shells were going to the Royal Navy, while the 16-inchers were for the U.S. I was amazed at the effort that was required to produce a 16-inch naval shell. Those things, after being machined inside and out, were then fitted with a machined copper band, and when standing up, were about five feet tall and weighed approximately 1,100 pounds.

Of course, none of the projectiles were loaded or fused at the Bethlehem Steel. That was a job for a munitions factory.

The Steel Company was filled with jokesters and, as might be expected, as an 18 year old new guy, I was prime bait for a lot of cute tricks. The shop was tremendously noisy, with all of the machinery going, and as I walked along, there would frequently be a guy who hollered "Yo!" but when I turned around, nobody was looking. After a while, I stopped turning around.

Then there were the wise guys who would ask, very seriously, "Hey, would you stop by the Tool Crib and get me six feet of Shore Line?" Or maybe it was a "Left Handed monkey wrench." etc. You had to wise up to those kinds of tricks quickly.

Bethlehem Steel was a dangerous place to work, and I soon found out that not looking around enough could be an unwise policy. The Shell Shop, like most of the other shops in the Bethlehem Steel, had an overhead bridge crane which ran the length of the shop. An operator sat in a box up on the crane and he could traverse not only the length of the shop but could also run a trunion back and forth laterally, in order to reach any place on the floor. Whenever the crane moved a bell clanged loudly, adding to the din, and there were constantly loads of steel moving back and forth overhead.

One day, while walking through the shop on one of my assigned errands I heard the clanging bell but did not pay it much attention. Suddenly, there was a tremendous BLAM accompanied by a blast of dirt-filled wind, which left me scrambling for cover!

I did not feel anything but my eyes were filled with dirt. When I finally got them cleared enough to see what happened I discovered that a 3-ton basket of 5-inch shells had dropped from the crane and hit the floor about 20 feet from where I was walking! Fortunately, the basket landed upright and the shells did not scatter.

Thereafter, I paid a lot more attention to crane bells and what was swinging overhead. The war was going in full swing and I was still waiting to be called up. It struck me as ironic to think that I might well have been killed by "friendly" shells before I got within 3,000 miles of the enemy!

Hitting the Treasury Balance

I must have been born lucky, because the falling shell incident was just one of many close shaves in my life. But not all my good fortune came in the form of near misses.

Although I have discussed it with many people, I have never met one who has ever heard of the Treasury Balance racket. Yet, in the forties everybody in the Bethlehem Steel, and I assume much of the Lehigh Valley, knew what it was. Basically, the daily Treasury Balance deal was a mob-run lottery in which you bought a ticket for 25 cents, 50 cents, or $1.00. You got a simple piece of paper stapled closed, and inside was a date and a six digit number.

The way it worked was as follows: Each day the U.S. daily Treasury Balance was posted in the newspaper, down to the last cent. (I assume it still is, but maybe since we are broke, they don't want to reveal it anymore.)

Anyway, ignoring the pennies, you checked your six-digit number against the last six digits in the daily Treasury Balance. If you hit various combinations, such as the first or last two or three, or all numbers scrambled, etc., you were paid off. If you were lucky enough to hit all six numbers, you hit a sizable payoff.

It was illegal, of course, and the mobsters made a good living at it, but it was small time stuff compared to the million-plus-dollar lotteries of today. No one was hurt badly and it was basically ignored by the authorities, who probably got a piece of the action anyway. Frankly, while the odds of a Treasury Balance hit were crummy I think they were a probably a lot better than the scams which are perpetuated by the multi-million Casinos and State-run lotteries today. However, I digress, so on with my story.

Every shop in Steel Company had one designated representative who sold the Treasury Balance tickets, and I occasionally bought one for 25 cents. One day I was casually checking my ticket and remarked, I have the first two, I have the first three – no four. Wow, I think I have all six. Unbelievable! Let me check that again. I was right – I hit all six numbers in a row, straight on – a 100,000 to 1 shot! All these years later I can still remember the number; it was 028920. I had won $1,000, a windfall in those days, when my monthly salary was just over $96, less Social Security, about 42 cents in those days.

Now, here is the interesting part. I showed my ticket to the guy who sold it to me. After checking the number he said, "OK, come over to my house Saturday morning for the payoff." He then gave me his address, which was only a few blocks from the Steel Plant shop where we worked.

On Saturday morning I showed up at his house and he introduced me to his wife and served me a cup of coffee while he made a phone call. We chatted for about 20 minutes until a long black limousine drove up in front of the house. Two guys looking every bit like movie-style mobsters were sitting in the car and didn't get out.

My host told me to go out to the car and show them my ticket. I noticed that he himself did not walk out to the car. No way was he going to risk being linked to the deal should any cops suddenly appear. As I approached the car, the guy in the front seat rolled down the window and, after scanning the surroundings carefully, asked to see the ticket.

He closely examined the number and the ticket, put the ticket in his pocket, and then, with me standing at his window, whipped out a stack of bills and proceeded to count out a grand's worth: $900 in one hundred dollar bills, and the last $100 in smaller bills to be used to tip the guy who sold me the ticket. Without another word the car rolled away and I went back into the ticket seller's house.

Scuttlebutt around the shop had been that the guy was expecting 10 percent, but I reasoned that it wasn't his luck, it was mine, and I wasn't likely to hit another 100,000 to 1 shot. I gave him 50 bucks and took off to enjoy my windfall.

I reflect with amusement on how the perspective on gambling has changed over the years. Today, you cannot legally play a $5.00 poker game in your own home, but gambling on a massive scale is OK and legal as long as the money lands in the correct pockets. Ironically, one of the steel company shops, about 1,000 feet from where I worked, has recently been converted into a massive Las Vegas-style casino, owned by the largest operator of casinos in Vegas, Steve Wynn.

"Hot Foots" on the Job

A couple of months after that job started somebody in the Steel Company, or maybe in the War Department, decided that they needed to establish a real effective communications system in the plants, so that in the event of an air raid, the word could be gotten to everyone quickly and appropriate measures taken.

Now here is the good part. Each of the Shops in the Steel Company was directed to set up an Air Raid Warning phone, which was manned 24 hours a day, on all work shifts, without fail. Guess who got to be the guy on my shift who sat every day watching the phone – me!

There was a little office right in the middle of the shop, and it had a desk and chair, a drinking fountain and a red telephone, which nobody was allowed to use for outgoing calls. Basically, I had to learn some procedures of whom to contact and in what order, etc, if the phone ever rang – which it never did. Other than that, my duties were exactly zero. I know that many people might term that their dream job – kind of like Vanna White having to turn over all those letters on "Wheel of Fortune," but her duties are infinitely more complex.

I might have enjoyed watching Vanna, but there wasn't any television in those days, so I read lots of books, and also slept a lot, leaning back in the chair with my feet on the desk. That proved to be one of the principal hazards of the job. Everybody in the plant had to wear steel-tipped safety shoes, including me. The guys from the floor would occasionally pop into my nook to get a cold drink of water, and of course when they spotted sleeping beauty they couldn't miss the opportunity. Every once in a while I would be awakened from my slumber by a red hot burning in my toes and would quickly dash to the fountain and pour water on my shoe. Some wise guy had stuck a match into the sole of my shoe and lighted it. That steel tip provided the perfect opportunity for a classic hot foot – plus!

After about six weeks of that arduous duty some astute individual in the War Department figured out that there wasn't any chance of the Bethlehem Steel Company getting bombed, as Hitler did not have a single airplane in his entire arsenal capable of even reaching the East Coast, let alone returning to Germany!

Chainman

The "Red Phone" was terminated and I was expected to move back to my Shop Clerk duties. However, that job was paying only $96 per month, and I still had quite a few months to wait before my call-up to active duty with the Air Corps, so I decided to see if I could get a job on the shop floor, where the pay was a bit more lucrative. I checked with Bethlehem Steel

Personnel and actually got transferred to another shop where they made all kinds of I beams and angle irons.

Every new worker in the Bethlehem Steel plant began as a basic Laborer, and the rate was $1.19 an hour, which sounds pretty grubby today, but was actually not bad pay then. Working five eight-hour days per week on a relentless round-the-clock swing shift I pulled down $95.20 per two week's pay, which was about twice what I got as a Shop Clerk. Not bad.

For the first week or so I pushed a broom and generally made myself useful. Then, suddenly a job opened up in the shop for a Chainman. That was a guy who hooked up and unhooked the loads of steel which were then transferred to other locations by the overhead cranes. I had seen those operations many times at my previous job and thought that didn't look so hard, so I asked for the job and got it. Maybe I should have asked where the last guy went, but I didn't. Besides, my pay took a shot up to $1.27 per hour. I was going up like a rocket.

There was a bit of technique associated with the job but I picked that up pretty quickly, with some advice from some old timers. There were various sizes of chains and tongs which you used to secure the load and you had to be careful to place them at a good balance point. The crane operator would lower the hoist; you attached the load carefully, got your hands clear, gave him the thumb-up signal to begin the hoist and stepped back out of the way. He would give it a short lift to check the balance, then move off, with crane bell clanging away.

Lowering loads and unchaining them was the reverse, but there were some definite no nos. For example , we used very heavy chains with huge links, so if you were up on top of a freight car unloading the steel you did not want to just toss the chain over the side, as those chains could whip back and really smack you hard. I saw that happen to a guy, who ran around with a bruised face for a week after he made that mistake.

As previously observed, the shop floor was a dangerous place to work and there were many accidents, some fatal. Everybody wore steel-tipped safety shoes and safety glasses, and we held Safety Meetings once or twice every week, with mandatory attendance. Nevertheless, there were a lot of real wacky guys working there and a lot of the accidents were the result of pure horseplay – guys playing tricks on each other.

For example, the shops had mostly earth floors and there were a lot of huge water beetles roaming around. I don't know where those things came from or what drew them to the steel shops, but I never saw big ones like that anywhere else. Maybe they liked the taste of steel or rust; who knows.

Those beetles were actually harmless, but they were about two inches long and looked pretty fierce, so some guys liked to get one and drop it down another guy's shirt. This resulted in people actually running around chasing one another in an environment where the floor was covered with razor sharp machining chips, and there were lots sharp steel angle irons which could gouge a leg to the bone. It was a nutty business.

One important rule in the chainman business was: When you remove the hook, sling, or tongs from the load after the crane operator lowers it into place, be sure to guide the attachment device away from any other obstacles before giving the signal to hoist.   One night while working the second shift (4 – 12 PM), we had a dramatic and tragic example of how accidents can happen when that rule is not strictly followed.

The shop in which I was working made very large I beams, many of which were bridge steel.   A typical beam might be 50 or more feet in length and when standing on its flange was about five feet high.   I don't know their exact weight but it was many tons. That night two chainmen, of which I was fortunately not one, were working with the crane operator to transfer the huge beams from inside the shop to a platform in the outside yard.   There they would await loading onto railroad cars on the nearby track.

For lifting I-beams we used a very large pair of tongs, which clamped over the flanges in the center of the I-beam.   The crane operator would lower the hook with tongs attached, the chain man would ask for enough slack to get the jaws of the tong over both sides of the flange, and then signal for a test lift. The crane operator would do a short lift to make sure that the tongs closed properly over both flanges and that the load was balanced.   If all was ok the chain man would give the thumbs up signal for the lift and away the crane and beam would go, with crane bell clanging loudly.

In the outside yard the chain man would do the reverse.   He would basically signal for a careful lowering, while guiding each beam into place on the platform in parallel rows, with several feet of space between the beams.   I don't know why but was told that the chain man was standing between an in-place beam and one he was lowering.   Perhaps it was near the end of

209

the platform.   In any case, the beam was lowered into place very carefully, and the chain man removed the tongs but allowed them to fall on the opposite side of the beam that had just been lowered.

He then gave the signal for the crane operator to raise the empty tongs. The tongs themselves would naturally close and there was no chance of them grasping anything, but there was a large nut which held the two sections of the tongs together and it caught on the flange of the beam and started tipping it toward the chain man. He saw the danger and tried to jump out of the way but one leg was caught and was instantly sheared off!

It was a terrible scene and I am glad I did not witness it.   It was also a sobering reminder of the unexpected manner in which danger can strike from a moment's carelessness when you are working with extremely heavy materials and powerful machinery.

The Four Dutchmen

I had one final job before I went into the military. I was always on the lookout for a better paying job in the shop, and the job I really had my eye on was overhead-crane operator.   I had established a good rapport with the crane operators in the shop, who must have concluded that I was pretty well coordinated and had demonstrated good sense as a chainman.   For whatever reason, one night on the 12 – 8 shift, when things were running a little slow, one of them invited me to climb the ladder into his cab, and started to teach me how to operate the crane.

It was quite interesting and challenging, as there was a lot of responsibility associated with a job where a single mistake could kill somebody.

After teaching me the basics of running the crane, he got into some of the finer points. One challenge was to learn how to take the swing out of a load. It was a pure coordination exercise, similarly to flying, where you were coordinating several dimensions of movement. Keep in mind that the crane could move back and forth the complete length of the shop, which was maybe 1000 feet or more. Also, the trunion could move back and forth across the width of the shop floor, and the hoist could move up and down.

To demonstrate, the operator hooked up a heavy beam, lifted it, then deliberately instigated a move which caused the load to start swinging. To dampen the swing, of course, you had to carefully move the controls so that you positioned the hoist over the center of the load, but you needed to anticipate the swing a bit while being careful not to over-control and aggravate the situation.

Another technique he taught me was how, after a good hoist had been achieved, to accelerate smoothly so as not to start a big swing, and then move at a constant speed keeping the load nicely centered. At the other end it was the reverse, slowing it carefully so you didn't end up with a pendulum that the chainman had to chase.

I knew that job paid well, and could have really gotten into it, as after several of those training sessions I was definitely a good candidate for the job. But those jobs were pretty much plums and the few guys that had them really hung on to them. An opening which appeared imminent never happened, so I remained in my ground job.

Then an odd thing happened. At the one end of our shop they had a special area where they painted the steel with red lead and other special protection coatings. One day the boss dropped the word that he was going to be putting on another spray painter, and wondered if anyone in the shop had any experience. Spray painter? That didn't sound so hot, as I remembered seeing the "Red Men" who made the paint (Chapter Three). However, I heard that those guys were some of the highest paid in the shop so I decided to check it out a bit.

Actually, I had done quite a bit of spray painting at our backyard garage, but that was spraying coatings of primer and lacquer to put fine finishes on motorcycles, using a one quart gun. I didn't know anything about industrial spray painting, so I went to the Public Library and checked it out. (No Internet then). It didn't look tough and I knew I could handle the job. Working around that stuff for a long time could be very risky, but I had only a few more months before call-up and thought, "Why not?"

I went to the boss and made a pitch. He had some reluctance, but apparently he didn't have any other candidates and said, "OK, I'll give you a try."

Now, here is where the whole deal gets almost comical. It turned out that there were four guys doing the painting, and they did not want the boss to bring in anybody else. Why? Believe it or not, those guys got paid on sort of a by-the-job/tonnage basis, (very irrational, and almost impossible to explain , so I won't try). But here is the real kicker - the pay for all of the work was put into one pot, which was split exactly four ways. Apparently the work load had increased and the boss was convinced he needed another painter, but they did not agree. In fact, they absolutely hated the idea. Not only were they going to be saddled with a brand new (slow) guy, but they were now going to have to split five ways!

To set the stage a bit, let me say that all four of those guys were skinny, about the same size (5' 8") and kind of resembled each other. Also, they were all Pennsylvania Dutchmen, who talked real "Dutchy", as the saying went. The analogy which kept coming to my mind was "like four pups from the same litter," but that it unkind, I guess.

Anyway, to get a true appreciation of the situation you would have had to see them work. Those guys were like a bunch of automatons hooked up to a machine that was running absolutely wild! They walked fast, sprayed frantically, and could spray in any direction, including behind their back, between their legs, and from underneath, probably with their eyes closed.

They could lay a swath of paint precisely at 20 feet or more, with never a miss. Sometimes when they would be working on a very large construction piece, such as a junction structure where a bunch of bridge steel beams came together, it was like watching an object rapidly turn red right before your eyes.

The equipment we used was a far cry from what I had used to paint motorcycles. To begin with, we each had a 30 gallon tank on wheels with castors and there were two long hoses hooked to the spray gun which we had to drag around and keep from getting hung up on beams or whatever. One hose contained the paint and the other was an air hose which we hooked to various high pressure air fittings which were scattered throughout the shop.

Those guys were not about to let the new slow guy get to any of the big stuff so they started me out on the most tedious small jobs, like angle irons. Those things were typically thirty of more feet in length and were laid out in rows on a series of low horses, with room for the painter to get in between. You would methodically work your way between the rows, spraying every surface in site, then, using a special steel bar, flip every angle iron over and repeat the process for the other, unpainted side.

Like every other job in the steel company there were special tricks and scams that you had to learn. For the painters, it had to do with the thickness of the paint. Typically, each steel contract had specifications for the color, type and thickness of the paint to be applied. However, if the paint was mixed to the specified thickness, it was like spraying with glue, so the Dutchmen would always slip in a couple of dippers of thinner whenever the boss was not looking. He frowned on that practice, but he knew it went on.

In fairness, I have to say that had they tried to spray to the specification it would have taken three times as long, and the result would not have been any better. As it was, the paint laid on very nicely and was quite adequate to the job. Those guys knew what they were doing and I soon learned to do the same.

What about safety equipment? We all know that working around red lead is dangerous. We had special, close fitting masks which kept us from breathing the stuff in, and wore safety shoes as well as safety glasses. One a month we were required to go for a special blood test, to insure that we were not getting poisoned by the stuff, a good idea. For clothing we wore blue jeans, long shirts, gloves and a cap.

After several days of spraying, our shoes would accumulate such a thick coating of paint we would slice it off with a putty knife. When we took off our pants they were stiff as a board and we could stand them against a wall. What did we do with them? Throw them away? You will hardly believe this, but we sent them to a local industrial laundry and they came back as soft as new jeans! I don't know what kind of solvents they used, but I never ceased to be amazed at that. For every challenge there is a solution.

After a month on the job, I was getting very fast, and approaching the end of the second month, I was almost as frantic as the four Dutchmen! Watching those guys work was a unique learning experience. I don't know whether one should conclude that it was a demonstration of the American work ethic. Rather, I think that it illustrates the principal, that "If applied correctly, money is the greatest incentive."

Off to War

In February 1943 I received orders to report to the Classification Center at Nashville, Tennessee, for the first phase of my military training. The early years in Bethlehem were over. It was time to move on with a new phase of life.

An End and a Beginning

After a 23 year career in the United States Air Force, Ed (on the right) now lives in Connecticut where he is CEO of Forecast International, a market research firm which provides long-range forecasts for the world's aerospace and defense industries.

216

Chapter Eleven

REFLECTIONS: LOOKING BACK

I didn't realize it at the time, but I was privileged to grow up in a splendid part of our great country during a special time in its history. While much of my early upbringing took place during the whole of the Great Depression, I do not have a single unhappy memory.

I know that my life exploring the bluebell-dotted meadows and navigating the mountains of the Lehigh Valley was a very special time which shaped my future in countless ways. It also provided a prelude to the momentous developments which took place in World War II, and were destined to impact almost everyone in my generation.

Quite frankly, I would do it all again.

Boredom and Depression – Never!

Today I often hear adults and young people complain about being bored. Some become so depressed that they commit suicide. This has become a problem of tragic proportion in today's society, and could stand some serious study.

As a kid growing up in Bethlehem and the surrounding towns, I never heard a single person, kid or adult, say that he or she was bored. No one really had any money, we did not live in fancy houses loaded with luxuries, and people were frequently out of work. But we were never at a loss for things to do, and even better, most of our amusements were free and unsupervised. There were no organized activities like little league then. If we wanted to play baseball, somebody found a ball and bat and we played in the street or an empty sandlot.

Oddly enough, this whole contradiction is set within the context of the word "depression." During the years 1929-1940, when I was 5-16 years old, our entire country was in the midst of that Great Depression, as it is termed in the history books. In the Lehigh Valley, we even had our own "Depression Beach," where hundreds of people swam free behind a dam and picnicked on the Monocacy Creek.

People may have been out of work but they weren't depressed; they simply accepted life as it was and made the best of it. Further, it was rare to hear anyone describe themselves as "poor," because everyone was in the same boat. In fact, people actually joked about it, and popular songs scoffed at it. We're in the Money from the musical 42nd Street summed up the feelings of many at the time. Its lyrics went:

We're in the money; we're in the money;

We've got a lot of what it takes to get along!

We're in the money, the skies are sunny;

Old man depression, you are through,

You done us wrong!

And then there was the standard by Gus Kahn and Harry Woods:

Oh, we ain't got a barrel of money,

Maybe we're ragged and funny

But we'll travel along

Singing a song

Side by side.

When my older sister was a teenager, she had a friend who had a beat-up old car with bald tires that had become so worn they had holes in them. Her friend inserted pieces of old tire over the holes to act as a shoe. Tires all had inner tubes in those days, so he was careful to always carry a patch kit and a tire pump when on the road.

One Sunday six of them spent an entire day riding around in that car, and suffered six flats along the way. My sister told me how they made a game of seeing how quickly they could jack up the car, pull off a wheel, pry the tube out of the tire (using tire irons), patch the tube, pump it back up, drop the jack, and get on their way. She came home laughing and said everyone had a great time.

I cannot help but think that maybe people today don't have enough challenges and spend too much time thinking about how bad their life is and what the government or somebody else should do for them instead of realizing the blessings they have in America, and just get busy.

Why Did The Bethlehem Steel Company Fail?

There have been many analyses of this subject, prepared by experts in every phase of Economics and Cost-Accounting, Management, Labor Relations, and other grand specialties. I will not attempt to criticize, interpret or comment on their findings, but I might as well toss in a few of my own conclusions, which are offered from what I like to consider a common sense standpoint, rather than an academic one.

My perspective is shaped on the basis of having viewed the workings of the Bethlehem Steel Company from several levels, top to bottom. Specifically, my father worked from the early 1920's through his retirement in the company headquarters and was in daily contact with top management figures. My brother and most of our friends worked in the plant in various jobs. My own experience included working for middle management in the shop offices, as well as on various jobs on the plant floor, starting from the very lowest level, common laborer. To round it out and perhaps provide balance, I was at one point a member of the Steelworkers Union, as I was working in a "Closed Shop" in which membership in the Union was required by prior agreement with management.

Many believe that the demise of Bethlehem Steel, and most of the rest of the American steel industry was inevitable, due to the shift in world industrial balances and labor economics, following World War II. Those events, including the Marshall Plan, which modernized the plants of our former enemies while our own languished, were certainly contributing factors, but I am not so sure that it could not have been otherwise. My own amateur analysis pinpoints some of the root causes for the failure as follows:

Communications,
Reporting and Personnel Management

There was a great gap in communications between upper management and the people at other levels of the plant. Middle Management in the plant shops reported to the front office and that was where its loyalty lay.

While these managers directed the daily operations in the plant from a technical standpoint they did not have much of a relationship with the workers on the floor, nor did they seem to have a clue as to how many sloppy and dangerous practices were being carried out almost right under their noses.

At the next level down, the Foremen of the various sections of the shops reported to the Middle Managers, frequently talking to them about routine operational problems in the various ongoing processes. However, I believe that the Foremen seldom communicated negative personnel actions to their bosses, as they were, in many cases, intimidated by the work force and the Union.

I observed this first hand, on many occasions, when foremen would weakly try to correct some sloppy or improper practices and were laughed at behind their backs by the workers. I think that in most cases these types of violations were not reported up the channels so that appropriate personnel action could be taken.

As for the workers themselves, by and large they were decent guys and good workers, but a significant portion seemed to spend more time trying to find ways to avoid work than would have been required to perform the work itself. I have related some of my observations in this regard. When observing these various scams and cagey practices, I sometimes wondered whatever happened to the old American adage, "A day's work for a day's pay." I think that many people never heard of this work ethic, or if they did, maybe they should revisit it.

Failure of the Union to Understand the Needs of its Industry

Leaders of the Steelworker's Union had little comprehension of the needs of a company to hold costs under control, and to help eliminate wasteful practices. Further, the thought that they should endeavor to help their employer to create a more efficient and more profitable work process was certainly not evident. Instead, there was the underlying viewpoint that the company was an omnipotent giant machine with endless resources and that they (the Union workers) were continually being victimized, even though they held the best paying jobs in the area.

I must add that this mentality certainly did not belong to everyone in the Union, as many workers were unwilling members, as I myself was. However, many did, in fact, exhibit continuing hostility to the company, and some were strongly influenced by Communist propaganda, unwittingly swallowing the line that Industry and Capital were their natural enemies, and should therefore be destroyed. I personally was handed a lot of that type of propaganda, while walking in or out of the gates at change-of-shift time.

It should be remembered that after June 1941 the Soviet Union was at war with Germany and was therefore our ally. Many times I observed signs in various storefronts and other places extolling the virtues of our gallant Soviet allies. I think it never occurred to those who found the Soviet economic system attractive that the industry they sought to destroy was a key one in supplying the Lend-Lease equipment that saved the Soviet Union from total defeat.

Failure of Top Management
to Look Beyond the Immediate Situation

The main focus of top management seems to have been upon how many contracts the company had "now" and the current degree of blackness of its bottom line on the Profit and Loss Statement. Whenever the Union demanded concessions and threatened to strike, or actually carried out a strike, the company was quick to grant concessions and settle, by simply raising the price of steel, as their greatest fear was a cessation of operations.

A careful study of what was happening in international steel markets and in the development of foreign plants with modernized steelmaking processes should have quickly made the handwriting on the wall clear, so that firm action for change could have taken place. Some efforts were made to modernize and to take back excessive concessions which had been granted, but they were typically too late.

Failure of the U.S. Government to Recognize the Coming Debacle

Overall, the policies of the U.S. Government in the years following WWII were a confused muddle of conflicting actions, and political jockeying . Everyone knew that America was the greatest industrial power in the world and arrogance prevailed. The common wisdom was, "It will always be that way. Hadn't we just proved it by flooding the world with defense equipment?" But wars have a way of changing the status quo.

A wise Government would have provided sweeping economic advantages for complete modernization of its heavy industry, included greatly accelerated depreciation and replacement allowances, as well as other tax advantages of many types, plus enhanced training programs for new industrial specialists. Even when the industrial dominos began to fall, there remained a mind-numbing lack of concern in Washington, and the prevailing thought seemed to have been, "What does it matter if our heavy industry declines? We can't expect to compete with their cheaper labor, etc.; we'll just switch to other technologies.

That actually happened to some extent, as America led the way in the computer revolution. But a great nation cannot let its industrial base vanish from its shores. Computers can design bridges, buildings and weapons, but they don't produce steel beams, armor plate and tanks. It is time for our leaders to wake up and face reality!

AFTERMATH

America entered World War II in December 1941, shortly before the author turned 18. Most of the people mentioned in this book were involved in the war in some way.

What happened to the author and some of his friends? A brief summation is provided below.

Cope, Charlie – Became high ranking executive in Bethlehem Steel Co.

Gieske, Neil – Joined the U.S. Navy and became a diver and underwater munitions disposal specialist.

Hill, Sheldon C. (Shelly) – Severely wounded while flying liaison and communications missions with the Army Air Corps, and spent a long time in VA hospitals after the war. Became a Bethlehem Steel executive. 32nd Degree Mason. Died in 2003

Jermyn, Percy – I have never seen him since my early flight training, but found a Percy Jermyn on the Internet, and assume it is the same. If so, he became a Major in the Army Air Corps. I do not know his assignments, but assume he became an important member of the Training Command, as his Flight Instructor skills were outstanding.

227

Kuhnsman, Paul – Aerial gunner on 8th Air Force B-17 in Germany. Shot down two enemy aircraft. Survived the war uninjured, but was later killed when a jack collapsed while he was working under a truck.

Nebinger, Bob – Top turret gunner on a B-25 bomber with the famous 345th Air Apaches group. Took part in campaigns in New Guinea and Pacific Islands. Survived a direct Kamikaze strike on his troop transport, and received a Bronze Star for his rescue efforts. Died 1976

Nebinger, Ed – Flew P-47 and P-51 fighters with 8th AF in Great Britain, and later flew a combat tour in Korea. Remained in USAF flying jets for the remainder of a 23-year Air Force career.

Nebinger, Frank M. – Father of the author. Died in 1952, one year after his retirement. Buried in Nisky Hill Cemetery, North Bethlehem, directly across the river from the Steel Company that he loved, with a spectacular view of the five remaining blast furnaces.

Nebinger, Helen (Mimi) – with Frank, above. Mimi lived to be 106 years old and was at one time the oldest person in the State of Connecticut, with a certificate from the Governor to prove it.

O'Hara, Bill – Merchant Marine service. Killed in 1944 when his gasoline tanker exploded in port, probably due to enemy sabotage.

Palmer, John – Unknown.

Rice, Frank – Served in the Pacific Island campaign as a combat Marine. Miraculously, survived half a dozen major battles, including Iwo Jima, without a scratch. Died in 1986

Rich, Stuart (Stu) – Unknown. Last contact with Rich was in Aviation Cadets at Nashville, Tennessee, in 1943.

Sachs, Eddie – Married Nancy McGarrity, a pretty girl from the North Street neighborhood. Killed at Indianapolis 500 race, 1964.

Schlicher, Kenneth (Kenny) - U.S. Navy.

Swope, Buddy – U.S. Navy

Tefs, Eddie – Became a B-24 flight instructor in U.S. Army Air Corps Training Command. Lives in Naples, Florida.

Thoma, Eddie – Killed by flak as copilot on 8th AF B-17 during a bombing mission over Germany, 1944.

Weaver, Ely – As B-25 tail gunner, was shot down, wounded and taken prisoner in Italy. Survived the war but later took his own life.

Werner, Elwood (Ellie) – Unknown.

Wirth, Russell – U.S. Navy during the war. Later became a shop Foreman at Bethlehem Steel.

Wray, Jack – Graduated Annapolis 1946. Became a leading genealogist. Lives in Phoenix, Arizona today.

Credits for Art Work and Photos

Cover Art/Photography

Cover Art - DA Visions Photography

Artwork by John J. Purdy Studios; Big Flats, NY

Curtiss "Jenny"

"Scrammy Junior"

Duesenberg, $75

Riding Backward

National Soaring Meet, Elmira, 1935

Crunch!

Fireworks Stand – Ka-Pow!

Walking the Railings

The Ventnor Elephant

Runaway 18 Wheeler

Cavalry Charge

Piper Cub on One Wheel

Photo Credits

Skyclone: Robert Reinbold

Slag dumping: Pennsylvania Museum of Steelmaking

Canal Lock: Pennsylvania Historical Society

Graf Zeppelin and Do.X: Deutsche Bundesarchive

Aviation Week/McGraw-Hill

U.S. Air Force

U.S. Navy

Library of Congress

Digicam History

Orchestra: Liberty High School, Bethlehem, PA

Hillclimber: Bikenet.com

Ford Trimotor: Aviation Week/McGraw-Hill

Friedensville Zinc Mine: Unknown

Roundhouse: Library of Congress

Icy Hill: Pennsylvania State Police

The cars: Library of Congress

Barn fire: Unknown

Fisher Body Strike (Cars turning over): Library of Congress